Will of Our Father

Atonement and Gospel Insights

FINAL UPDATE - December 2020

LaVelle Day, All Rights Reserved

© 2009, 2018, 2020

This book is dedicated to
my wife, Marie and our extended family

Acknowledgements

My wife, Marie, has spent considerable time in doing some reviewing of this publication and being patient while I work on it, for which I am extremely grateful. Judy Day provided the expertise and time in creating the book cover. The book cover could not be better. It is personally very satisfying.

This book has gone through multiple revisions. It seems that there was always something that needed to be added, revised to accurately explain my analysis or some statement by the prophet Joseph Smith that further explained some concept.

As the manuscript kept changing, many different people contributed comments to better explain my thoughts. I thank them all and I indeed am grateful for their contributions.

At the beginning President Lloyd Campbell, my stake president, was aware of my continued development and gave me positive encouragement and feedback.

But the person who helped me to finalize this final publication is my daughter-in-law. Debbilyn Day. She questioned my initial writings which required me to add additional quotes to provide a stronger starting basis for some of my analytical thoughts. In addition, she taught me the structural details that I needed to publish the book according to professional standards.

Author's Purpose

My research began with a desire to understand the atonement and the plan of salvation. As I read various books and the scriptures of the Church, I started making notes and stored them in separate topical format. I was very interested in understanding the plan of salvation.

I have a special promise in my patriarchal blessing telling me that I would "fully understand the plan of Salvation." It is contained in the first paragraph of my patriarchal blessing. Initially no thought of publishing was considered. Eventually I felt that I had something of value with answers to many of my questions and that perhaps others might benefit from what I had collected. So, I decided to publish my research in a book.

Many quotes from the scriptures, Church related publications, historical publications and the internet are included. Researching Joseph Smith quotes was a priority.

By including these references, the readers can evaluate the accuracy of the material contained in this book.

ABOUT THE AUTHOR

LaVelle Day grew up in Utah and Eastern Oregon, one of four children. He became active in the Church of Jesus Christ of Latter-day Saints when a high school junior. He served a mission in the California Mission, married Marie Nielsen and graduated from Brigham Young University with a BS degree in mathematics and minor in English. He spent one year at Utah State University as a mathematics teaching assistant and doing graduate work.

He started his working career with IBM as a system engineer followed by increasing responsibilities at other companies. During this time, he obtained his law degree from Lewis and Clark Law School evening program and passed the Oregon State Bar following graduation. After this, he managed a local office of an international company providing supplemental staff and consulting in Portland, Oregon, where he earned high performance awards.

LaVelle and Marie have five children and 16 grandchildren. His most cherished and anticipated times are bi-annual week-long family reunions.

LaVelle has served in multiple positions within the Church including several stake missions, high councilman (multiple times), bishop counselor (twice), bishop, employment office manager and Portland transient services bishop.

He and his wife, Marie, spent 18 months in Pottsville, Pennsylvania as Utah Genealogical Society representatives to collect records from churches, funeral homes, cemeteries and libraries. To obtain contracts, a self-developed PowerPoint presentation educated interested parties on records preservation, which produced pleasing results. Our mission was dedicated to getting contracts, not filming. Others did the actual capture of the records.

PREFACE

The goal of this book is to address principles of the plan of salvation, which include atonement and gospel principles not commonly understood. The book is intended to engage readers of all levels.

Quotes from Joseph Smith were researched and used in explaining important aspects of the atonement and gospel principles discussed. Quotes are broad and include more than the important points to provide reference context. However, the reader should focus on the bolded or underlined parts because these are the concepts that are being discussed.

This book is a technical read, due to the many scriptures and quotes used. Unless the reader understands the concepts contained in the quotes, they will struggle with understanding some of the following points made in the book.

Some Major Points are:

- Identifies exactly what caused the Savior's suffering in the Garden. This is not normally understood.
- Shows that the Savior shed all of his blood out of his body in the Garden and became immortal. He was immortal during his maltreatments and cross sufferings.
- Identifies the bitter cup suffered by the Savior.
- Explains maltreatments not often considered.
- Identifies separate groups of spirits in the world of spirits and their eventual or possible habitation in eternity.
- Explains the need of babies and small children to develop following their resurrection and how this is done.
- Explains the marriage covenant, and the eternal status of those who reject this covenant.
- Explains the qualification and status of sons of perdition showing many will qualify. Surprising!
- Explains the Law of Moses and associated priesthood key issues.
- Explains why Peter denied Christ three times.

The important parts of any quotes used in this book are bolded or <u>underlined</u>. These are the points important to the current discussion. Reference to the Garden of Gethsemane is generally shortened to Garden. Reference to God, our Heavenly Father is mostly used as Father. Quotations containing spelling or current language errors are not corrected but are provided as contained in the quoted material.

Importance of our English Language

The Lord made this statement in the first revelation printed in the current version of the Doctrine and Covenants,

> *Behold, I am God and have spoken it; these commandments are of me, and were given unto my servants in their weakness, after the manner of their language, that they might come to understanding.*[1]

The language mentioned in this statement by the Savior is our English language. When Joseph Smith received revelations which were recorded, they were recorded in our English language.

English dictionaries have been used to provide meaning of various words to provide a better understanding of what a scriptural expression actually means. Understanding of common usage of our language gives meaning to the expressions used in the scriptures.

---

[1] D&C 1:24

TABLE OF CONTENTS

Author's Purpose	3
ABOUT THE AUTHOR	4
PREFACE	5
■WILL OF OUR FATHER■	11
■ ATONEMENT PLAN ■	14
MORTALITY	14
RESURRECTION - IMMORTALITY	14
George Laub Recording	17
CHRIST – COMPLETING HIS PROMISES	18
Completing His Ministry	19
Completing His Atonement	20
RECEIVING ALL POWER	21
Exercising All Power	22
CHRIST'S LOVE	22
■ ATONEMENT SUFFERINGS ■	25
HISTORICAL PUNISHMENTS	25
SCOURGING	25
CRUCIFIXION	25
GETHSEMANE	28
Definition of These Things	29
Suffering These Things	30
Father's Presence	34
Becoming Immortal	34
His Greater Suffering	37
MALTREATMENTS	37
Being Immortal - Suffering Pain	38
Arrest, Trial and Maltreatments	38
His Cross Pains	43

Cause of His Death	46
Decision to Die	47
Final Moments	49
Re-Suffering Gethsemane?	50
State of His Body	51
BITTER CUP	51
SUFFERING PEOPLE PAINS?	53
Emotion	55
One Emotion	56
Savior's Emotion	60
Suffering Alone	62
∎SALVATION OF MORTALS∎	64
BAPTISM	65
FORGIVENESS	65
Maintaining Forgiveness	66
Perfection and Sin	67
INFINITE ATONEMENT	70
MARRIAGE COVENANT	70
The Covenant	71
Lord's Law	73
Ministering Servants	74
Section 131	76
Section 22 and Marriage Covenant	76
Marriage Covenant Children	77
Posterity	78
Our Wayward Posterity	80
PROBATIONARY LIFE	82
ETERNAL LIFE	83
Progression	84

WORLD of SPIRITS	84
The Wicked	86
Group 1	86
Group 2	89
The Rebellious	90
Everlasting Fire	94
No Knowledge of Truth	96
Honorable Men/Women	98
Buffetings of Satan	99
Savior's Teaching and Organization	103
Just Men Made Perfect	104
Little Children	106
Children Resurrection	110
ANGER – PERFECTION	111
Tool of Satan	111
Nephi's Anger	114
Savior's Anger?	117
John' Temple Cleansing	118
James E Talmage View	121
TEMPLE CLEANSING	122
Temple Ordinance Status	122
One Cleansing	124
Savior's Challenge	125
SINS OF THE WORLD	125
Kingdoms, Dominions and Glory	128
SONS OF PERDITION	131
Qualifications	131
Murder – Shedding Innocent Blood	134
David's Murder of Uriah	137

Holy Ghost – Denying Christ	140
Sherem	140
Korihor	141
Nehor	142
Lamanite Converts	142
Knowing God's Power	143
THE MILLENNIUM	148
Consuming Fire	148
Mortality	149
All Resurrections	150
Resurrected Babies	152
Final Judgment	153
■ OTHER SUBJECTS of INTEREST ■	156
LAW OF MOSES	156
Elijah and the Temple Keys	161
What Priesthood Authority Remained?	166
The Dilemma – No Sealing Keys	167
The Solution	168
PETER DENYING CHRIST	171
Messiah Understanding	172
Peter Defending the Savior	175
Being Converted	179
DETERMINING PASSOVER EVENTS	180
■ ATONEMENT PERSPECTIVES ■	184
■ BIBLIOGRAPHY ■	186

■WILL OF OUR FATHER■

Our Father in heaven loves us - his spirit children. He wanted us to be like he is. However, we needed to grow and develop our own knowledge, skills and talents. He recognized that we as spirit children needed to have a physical body that our spirits could inhabit. He also knew that we needed an example we could follow that would help us to be like him. That example was Jesus Christ who lived perfectly. The Father gave the Savior direct responsibility for all the people that would live on this earth. He will determine where each of us we be in eternity. He is the Savior and Redeemer of this world.

Jesus Christ was the first spirit child born to our Father in Heaven,

> *And now, verily I say unto you,* ***I was in the beginning*** *with the Father, and* ***am the Firstborn.***[2]

At the very beginning, the Father began teaching Jesus Christ to be our Savior. This was confirmed to Moses who was told,

> *...behold, my Beloved Son, which was my Beloved and Chosen from the beginning*[3]

Our Father in Heaven received a proposal from another spirit child, Satan, who proposed,

> *Behold, here am I, send me, I will be thy son, and I will redeem all mankind, that one soul shall not be lost, and surely I will do it; wherefore give me thine honor.*[4]

Satan knew that Christ was chosen to be the Savior of this world and he wanted to replace him. He wanted to be the Savior. By promising to see that not one child would be lost, Satan thought that God would accept his proposal. Satan recognized the Father's great love for all his children and that he wanted them to become like himself.

After Satan made his proposal, the Savior promised the Father:

> *Father, thy will be done, and the glory be thine forever.*[5]

---

[2] D&C 93:21
[3] Moses 4:2
[4] Moses 4:1
[5] Moses 4:2

Satan's proposal was refused. The Father explained his rejection,

> Wherefore, because that **Satan rebelled against me, and sought to <u>destroy the agency of man</u>, which I, the Lord God, had given him,** and also, that I should give unto him mine own power; by the **power of mine Only Begotten, I caused that he should be cast down**;[6]

God gave the agency or the ability to make choices to man.

Satan was cast out of heaven. He was very influential among the spirit children of the Father. This is shown in a revelation to Joseph Smith and Sidney Rigdon,

> And this we saw also, and bear record, that an **angel of God <u>who was in authority</u>** in the presence of God, **who rebelled against the Only Begotten Son** whom the Father loved and who was in the bosom of the Father, was thrust down from the presence of God and the Son,

> And <u>was called Perdition</u>, **for the heavens wept over him—he was Lucifer, a son of the morning.**

> And we beheld, and lo, he is fallen! is fallen, even a son of the morning![7]

Satan was so influential that a third of Father's spirit children followed Satan and were cast out with him to the earth. This happened prior to Adam and Eve being placed in their Garden.[8] The evil that is upon the earth comes from Satan and his followers. They have the ability to tempt people to do evil things. Satan tempts evil people to tempt other people to do evil things that destroys what the Savior is trying to accomplish.

To show the true character of Satan, Moses wrote of his experience with Satan:

> I will not cease to call upon God, I have other things to inquire of him: for his glory has been upon me, wherefore I can judge between him and thee. <u>Depart hence, Satan.</u>

---

[6] Moses 4:3
[7] D&C 76:25-27
[8] Revelation 12:4

*And now, when Moses had said these words, <u>Satan cried with a loud voice, and ranted upon the earth</u>, **and commanded, saying: I am the Only Begotten, worship me.***[9]

This desire to control and have everyone worship him is what drives Satan to fight against God and to tempt humankind. If he can get humankind to accept his temptations, then they become subject to him and under his control. The extreme of this influence is when people become Sons of Perdition.

The Father reconfirmed that Jesus Christ would be his Only Begotten Son and the Savior of the world. At the time the Father made this decision, he confirmed that humankind would have their agency to make choices. They would not be forced to follow his commandments.[10] Our freedom to choose was guaranteed in heaven before we even came to earth.

---

[9] Moses 1:18-19
[10] Moses 4:3, Moses 7:32

ATONEMENT PLAN

The concepts of mortality and immortality are important to gain a better understanding of the Garden of Gethsemane events and sufferings later experienced by the Savior. This section addresses events that made the Savior our judge and king and finishes by showing the great love of the Savior to complete his atonement for us as his siblings.

MORTALITY

Blood is essential to a living physical body. It performs many functions relating to mortal life including:

- carrying needed oxygen and nutrients throughout the body
- carrying waste products back to the lungs, kidneys and liver for disposal
- attacking infections and helping to heal wounds

Generally, our body develops until it is at its peak performance. Then it gradually starts to deteriorate, perhaps at different rates, but we age. When we are old, our bodies become frail, our skin becomes thin and we bruise easily. We develop ailments such as diabetes, arthritis, atherosclerosis, heart or liver problems, etc. No one is immune from the aging process although some deteriorate faster than others. Eventually a critical part of our body fails and we die.

When a person dies, the heart stops beating and blood ceases to flow through the veins. This starts the decaying process which generally progresses rather rapidly. In fact, many states have or have had regulations stating that the body needs to be buried or cremated within a short period of time unless it is embalmed. During the embalming process, blood is removed from the body and replaced with an embalming fluid. This fluid helps the dead body to be preserved.

At death, there is a separation of our spirit and our mortal body. Our bodies remain with mother earth in various states and our spirits go to the world where all spirits go, which is here on this earth

RESURRECTION - IMMORTALITY

All mortals will be resurrected. We will have bodies just like we now have only they will be whole and complete in every particular including the hair of our heads.[11] Our bodies will be immortal, that is we are not subject to death any more.

The fundamental principle of the resurrection is,

> *The soul shall be restored to the body, and the body to the soul; yea, and every limb and joint shall be restored to its body; yea, even a hair of the head shall not be lost; but all things shall be restored to their proper and perfect frame.*[12]

Just how our physical bodies are made whole and perfect is not known, but it is done by the power of God. There are some whose bodies are not buried. There are some who have been cremated, maimed, lost at sea or eaten by animals. We know that God, the creator, has all power and will provide bodies just like the ones we had on earth for our spirit to inhabit.

Our mortal bodies are corruptible and subject to aging and eventual death. When the scriptures talk about corruption putting on incorruption, it refers to our mortal bodies becoming immortal and not subject to death. This occurs with our resurrection. Our resurrected bodies become immortal, not subject to aging and death.

What causes a body when it is resurrected to not die again?

We know that our physical bodies will be resurrected and will be complete and whole, but what will be the change to make it immortal?

The prophet Ezekiel was shown a vision about the resurrection. It started by showing Ezekiel a valley of dry bones,

> *And he said unto me, Son of man, can these bones live? And I answered, O Lord God, thou knowest.*

> *Again he said unto me, Prophesy upon these bones, and say unto them, O ye dry bones, hear the word of the Lord.*

> *Thus saith the Lord God unto these bones;* **Behold, I will cause breath to enter into you, and ye shall live***:*

---

[11] Alma 11:44
[12] Alma 40:23

> *And I will lay sinews upon you, and will bring up flesh upon you, and cover you with skin, and put breath in you, and ye shall live; and ye shall know that I am the Lord.*[13]

Ezekiel was shown in vision the resurrection of our bodies. Then the Lord continued,

> *And ye shall know that I am the Lord, when I have opened your graves, O my people, and brought you up out of your graves, And shall put <u>my spirit in you</u>, and ye shall live.*[14]

Then the Lord specifically states that he will "*put my spirit in you.*" The word spirit has so many different meanings that it is difficult to determine what the expression "*my spirit*" in this quote really means. Joseph Smith made several comments on this spirit in the body during the last years of his life.

On Sunday March 20, 1842, Wilford Woodruff recorded in his journal quoting Joseph Smith, which Joseph approved,

> *As concerning the resurrection, I will merely say that all men will come from the grave as they lie down, whether old or young; there will not be "added unto their stature one cubit," neither taken from it;* **all will be raised by the power of God, <u>having spirit in their bodies</u>, and <u>not blood</u>.**[15]

Though not specifically stated, this statement does suggest that spirit replaces blood. It has some relational connection.

From a talk by Joseph Smith on May 12, 1844, there were two brethren who made a record of it. Both recorded the message in different words. Joseph talked about the resurrection, having spirit in the body and no blood, but the message was recorded very differently. One brother was Thomas Bullock, Joseph's clerk. He recorded the following,

> *God Almighty Himself dwells in eternal fire; flesh and blood cannot go there, for all corruption is devoured by the fire. "Our*

---

[13] Ezekiel 37:3-6
[14] Ezekiel 37:11-14
[15] Smith, History of the Church, 4:556

God is a consuming fire." **When our flesh is quickened by the Spirit, there will be no blood in this tabernacle.**[16]

His record on this date was recorded in the History of the Church.

George Laub Recording

George Laub recorded the same sermon in his journal,

> *Concerning Resurrection <u>Flesh and Blood cannot inherit the kingdom of god or the kingdom that god inherits</u> or inhabits.* ***But the flesh without the blood and the spirit of god flowing in the vains in Sted of the blood*** <u>*for blood is the part of the body that causes corruption.*</u> *Therefore we must be changed in the twinkling of an eye or have to lay down these tabernacles and leave the blood vanish away. Therefore Jesus left his blood to atone for the sins of the world that he might assend into the presence of the Father for God dwells in flaming flames and he is a consuming fire he will consume all that is unclean and unholy and we could not abide his presence ;unless pure spirits in us. for the Blood is the corruptible part of the tabernacles.* [17]

George Laub's record is much more detailed. Can it be relied upon?

Thomas Bullock was Joseph's clerk and had recorded many of the prophet's talks. In past talks Joseph is quoted by Thomas Bullock as saying *"When our flesh is quickened by the spirit, there will be no blood in this tabernacle."* Thomas Bullock recorded these statements and being familiar with the concept would use the language he has written previously regardless of what was actually spoken by Joseph. He repeated what he had recorded several times.

However, George Laub was new to recording the prophet's talks. Being new he would be more attentive in recording exactly what the prophet said. He was not familiar with what Joseph was recorded as saying in his past talks. So, his record is more reliable than that of Thomas Bullock's record. It is much more detailed. Also, the chances of him making up the writings of his record, if Joseph never spoke them, are nil. How could he make up these comments, if they were never spoken by Joseph Smith? George Laub's record is very reliable

---

[16] History of the Church Vol 6, Ch 17, P 363; See also Words of Joseph Smith, P 368

[17] The Words of Joseph Smith, P 370-371

as being spoken by Joseph Smith and will be used as a reliable source in this book.

One important part of George Laub's quote is that God's spirit, which is identified as being in a resurrected body, replaces blood! It is a fluid and circulates throughout the entire body providing the immortality of the body.

Continuing

When Adam and Eve partook of the forbidden fruit, their bodies changed from being immortal to being mortal. The forbidden fruit caused the spirit flowing through their veins to change to blood, which all of us inherited. They began having children populating the earth.

It should be noted that Ezekiel quoted God as saying he (God) *"shall put **my spirit in you**"* to make these bodies live. We now know that this spirit replaced blood and it is God's spirit that is placed there. God has a substance identified as spirit flowing through the veins of his body that makes him immortal.

During the millennium, all mortal bodies will be changed from this mortal state to a resurrected state in the *"twinkling of an eye,"*

> *And he that liveth when the Lord shall come, and hath kept the faith, blessed is he; nevertheless, it is appointed to him to die at the age of man.*
>
> *Wherefore, children shall grow up until they become old; old men shall die; but they shall not sleep in the dust, but they shall be changed in the <u>twinkling of an eye</u>.*[18]

So, old men and women will become immortal in the twinkling of an eye. To become immortal, spirit replaces blood in their bodies. Think of it! In an instant blood is replaced by spirit. In addition, all of their body parts will function perfectly.

CHRIST – COMPLETING HIS PROMISES

This section will focus on the Savior's promises to the Father. Generally stated the Savior would do all things necessary to provide the resurrection for all of Father's children who would come to this

---

[18] D&C 63:50-51, See also D&C 43:32, 63:51, 101:31

earth. In addition, he promised the Father that the honor and glory would be his.

Completing His Ministry

Before we came to this earth, Satan proposed that he would make it so that everyone would return to the presence of the Father. Satan would take away our agency and force us to follow the Father's commandments.

A previous quote that shows the Savior's commitment to the Father, states,

> But, behold, my Beloved Son, which was my Beloved and Chosen from the beginning, said unto me—**Father, thy will be done, and the glory be thine forever.**[19]

John records the Savior's intercessory prayer which followed the Last Supper. In it the Savior said,

> I have glorified thee on the earth: **I have finished the work which thou gavest me to do.**[20]

This quote refers to his work, which was his ministry. His atonement sufferings would begin shortly. In his intercessory prayer, he followed with these words,

> I have manifested thy name unto the men which thou gavest me out of the world: thine they were, and thou gavest them me: and **they have kept thy word.**
>
> Now **they have known that all things whatsoever thou hast given me are of thee.**
>
> For I have given unto them the words which thou gavest me; and they have received them, and **have known surely that I came out from thee, and they have believed that thou didst send me.**[21]

In this prayer the Savior states that he gave all the honor and recognition of what he did in his ministry to the Father.

Following the Passover meal and prior to the intercessory prayer, the Savior told his disciples that he would leave them to return to the

---

[19] Moses 4:2
[20] John 17:4
[21] John 17:6-8

Father and they would feel sorrow. Then they would see him again and they would rejoice. To this comment the apostles replied,

> *Now are we sure that thou knowest all things, and needest not that any man should ask thee:* **by this we believe that thou camest forth from God.**[22]

This was their acknowledgement that the Savior was sent from the Father to do his work. The Savior fulfilled his promise that the honor and glory would be the Father's. He fully taught that he represented the Father and that all things were done according to the Father's will. This is confirmed by the apostles' statement that "*we believe that thou camest forth from God.*"[23] However, at that time the apostles did not understand the Savior's mission of the atonement and resurrection, but they truly believed that the Savior taught the will of the Father.

Completing His Atonement

Following that prayer, John records that they crossed over the brook Cedron to the Garden of Gethsemane. John does not record the Garden prayer nor his pain and bleeding. Matthew, Mark and Luke have done a good job in substantiating this event.

The Savior still had to fulfill the commandment of the Father to lay down his life and take it up again to provide the resurrection.[24] It was possible that the Savior might not fulfill this commandment. The Savior had his agency for he said the following about his suffering the "bitter cup,"

> *and would that I might not drink the bitter cup,* **and shrink-**[25]

If the Savior shrinks from the bitter cup, then he would not fulfill his commitment to the Father. However, he fulfilled that commitment. He stated to the Nephites when he appeared to them that he had drank the bitter cup,

---

[22] John 16:30
[23] John 16:30
[24] John 10:17-18
[25] D&C 19:18

Behold, I am Jesus Christ, whom the prophets testified shall come into the world.

*And behold, I am the light and the life of the world; and **I have drunk out of that bitter cup which the Father hath given me,** and have glorified the Father in taking upon me the sins of the world, in the which I have suffered the will of the Father in all things from the beginning.*[26]

The Savior held true to his commitment to the Father by enduring the bitter cup. The Savior chose to complete the atonement which provided the resurrection for all humankind and salvation for all but the sons of perdition.

RECEIVING ALL POWER

This section discusses the fact that the Savior was given all power by the Father and what that power entails.

John's writings shed some light on this concept of receiving all power. Part of John's record was given by direct revelation as found in the Doctrine and Covenants,

And I, John, bear record that he received a fulness of the glory of the Father;
*And he **received all power, both in heaven and on earth**, and the glory of the Father was with him, for he dwelt in him,* [27]

When his atonement was finished, he then received a *"fulness of glory"* and then he received all power in heaven and earth, [28]

Following his resurrection, the Savior met the eleven apostles at a mountain in Galilee and confirmed to his apostles that he received "all power" following his resurrection. Matthew records the Savior as saying to the eleven apostles,

All power is given unto me in heaven and in earth. [29]

---

[26] Nephi 11:10-11
[27] D&C 93:16-17
[28] D&C 93:17
[29] Matthew 28:18

The expression "is given unto me" indicates that the power was recently given to him. When the Savior was resurrected by re-inhabiting his body and Mary saw him in the Garden, he told Mary,

> *Touch me not: for I am not yet ascended to my Father: but go to my brethren, and say unto them, I ascend unto my Father, and your Father; and to my God, and your God.*[30]

When he returned to the Father, the Father gave him all power. By this authority, he became our advocate, Savior and king.

Exercising All Power

Since Christ is our judge it seems appropriate to mention in this section positive and negative judgments that he may make. He has identified courses of action that he can choose to exercise,

> *Hearken, O ye people, and open your hearts and give ear from afar; and listen, you that call yourselves the people of the Lord, and hear the word of the Lord and his will concerning you.*
>
> *Yea, verily, I say, hear the word of him <u>whose anger is kindled against the wicked and rebellious;</u>*
>
> **Who willeth to take even them whom he will take, and preserveth in life them whom he will preserve;**
> **Who buildeth up at his own will and pleasure; and destroyeth when he pleases, and is able to cast the soul down to hell.**
>
> <u>Behold, I, the Lord, utter my voice, and it shall be obeyed.</u>[31]

The Lord is very active in the affairs of this world but does not control or dictate what we do personally. We have our agency to choose what we do. He may bless us for the choices we make or he may hedge up our way making progress difficult depending upon what kind of choices we make. In fact, he can cause our lives to be taken, if he chooses.

CHRIST'S LOVE

Probably the most obvious activities that demonstrate the Savior's love for humankind is his ministry, wherein he performed the many

---

[30] John 20:17
[31] D&C 63:1-5.

miracles of healing. They are obvious because many witnessed these miracles as he performed them. We have no record of all of these miracles, but the Savior's reputation of being a healer was widely known.

One such event, recorded by Matthew, Mark and Luke[32] describes a man who had palsy which confined him to a bed. He was brought to the Savior and the multitude was so great that the Savior could not be reached. His friends took the afflicted man to the roof of the building, opened the roof and let him down so that the Savior could minister to him. The Savior recognized the faith of the invalid man and stated that his sins were forgiven. Attendant scribes viewed within themselves that the Savior was being blasphemous. The Savior understood their thoughts and chastised them. Then the Savior healed the man and told him to take up his bed and return to his home. This demonstrated that the Savior had the power to forgive sins as well as heal people.

The multitude was astonished at this miracle. All three gospels record that the multitude "glorified God" and had not seen such miracles. This is an example of his reputation. The popularity of Christ with the people was very strong. This is also illustrated by his entry into Jerusalem at Passover time.[33] Matthew, Mark and John describe this event in similar terms. John records that many came to see Lazarus, whom Jesus had recently raised from the dead. All of these people had seen or heard stories about the Savior's healing powers. He was recognized by some as did Nicodemus, who said the Savior was a,

> *teacher come from God: for no man can do these miracles that thou doest, except God be with him.*[34]

The Savior ministered and blessed the people because of his great love for them. He did not come to judge during his earthly ministry as he told the adulteress, *"Neither do I condemn thee: go, and sin no more."*[35]

---

[32] Matthew 9:2-8, Mark 2:1-12, Luke 5:18-26
[33] Matthew 21:1-11, Mark 11:1-10, John 12:9-15
[34] John 3:2
[35] John 8:11

Probably one of the greatest statements of his love for his brothers and sisters is,

> *Greater love hath no man than this, that a man lay down his life for his friends.*[36]

This statement was referring to his love for all his siblings, knowing that he would be laying down his life to complete his atonement.

Most Christian people quote this statement as it relates to war and other events, when individuals perform some heroic action preserving the lives of others.

One of the most emotional showings of the Savior's love is when he first visited the Nephites and Lamanites. He healed them with miracles and then prayed with and for them,

> *And they arose from the earth, and he said unto them: Blessed are ye because of your faith. And now behold, my joy is full.*
>
> *And **when he had said these words, he wept**, and the multitude bare record of it, and he took their little children, one by one, and blessed them, and prayed unto the Father for them.*
>
> *And when he had done this **he wept again**;*[37]

His weeping was from his joy and love for those present. He has the same love for us as we follow him and his teachings. His love for us is very real.

---

[36] John 15:13
[37] 3 Nephi 17-20-22

ATONEMENT SUFFERINGS

The Savior suffered many things in the process of providing his atonement. As previously stated, he told the Nephites that he suffered the bitter cup, which the father required. Before proceeding with this discussion, some historical information will be provided.

HISTORICAL PUNISHMENTS

Corporal punishment has existed from ancient times to very recent times and was used throughout the world. It was not centered in any one area and the type of punishment varied.

There are two punishments of great interest. They are scourging and crucifixion. These are of interest because the Savior suffered from both.

SCOURGING

Historically, the tool used in scourging was a whip with several leather straps. Sometimes the straps were laced with bone and metal with small lead balls at the end. The victim was tied low to a post so that they were bent over or tied high to stretch them up. There was no limit to the number of lashes. The contemporary historians, Livy, Suetonius and Josephus, have written of scourging cases where victims died while still bound to the post. Scourging was referred to as "half death."[38]

Although the Jewish law restricted the lashes to 40, the Romans inflicted the punishment, and sometimes were not restricted. The lashes from the scourging would make a massive wound with bruises from the shoulders to buttock and sometimes lower. Criminals and slaves were mainly the ones punished with scourging.

CRUCIFIXION

Several ancient civilizations punished people with crucifixion. The Romans began using crucifixion about 600 BC and was probably borrowed from the Carthaginians. The crosses that were used consisted of the post, patibulum and sometimes a sedile or seat. The

---

[38] https://en.wikipedia.org/wiki/Flagellation#Antiquity. From Antiquity Section Last visited June 2020

patibulum or crosspiece was rested on the top of the post or down from the top a very short distance.

The Romans prolonged the death of a victim as much as possible because they wanted the victim's suffering to act as a deterrent. Providing a "sedile" or a place to sit would give the victim rest and would lengthen the time to die. Zias, author of the article "Crucifixion in Antiquity" quotes Quintilian who wrote,

> *whenever we crucify the guilty, the most, crowded roads are chosen, where most people can see and be moved by this fear. For penalties relate not so much to retribution as to their exemplary effect.*[39]

Many people are generally knowledgeable about Spartacus, a slave gladiator, who escaped with about 70-80 other gladiators. Eventually they raised an army estimated from 80,000 to over 100,000 men who were mostly slaves. After a number of successes this army was defeated about 71 BC. Most were killed. A few escaped, but about 6,000 of the army were captured and crucified. They lined the Appian Way and were left on their crosses for a long period of time following their death. This was a lingering reminder to the general population of what they would experience, if they fought against the Romans.

A number of ancient authors have described crucifixion as being an extremely tortuous and painful death. The following quote illustrates this,

> Cicero called crucifixion the *'extreme and ultimate punishment of slaves' (*servitutis extremum summumque supplicium, Against Verres 2.5.169*), and the 'cruelest and most disgusting penalty.' (*crudelissimum taeterrimumque supplicium, ibid. 2.5. 165.) and **Josephus call it "the most pitiable of deaths."** (Jewish War 7:203.) [40]

---

[39] Zias "Crucifixion in Antiquity" P 7, Zias Ref: Quintilian   [AD 35-95) Decl 274 Internet Link is
https://web.archive.org/web/20110615201341/
http://www.centuryone.org/crucifixion2.html. Last visited June 2020

[40] Bible history online: The Roman Scourge; Link was Last visited June 2020
    http://www.bible-history.com/past/flagrum.html
- quote is beneath the picture with "Flagellum, Symbol of Sol" Under it.

If a person was crucified following scourging, they only lived a very short time. The scourging would hasten their death on the cross if they lived through the scourging.

People feared greatly at being crucified. Josephus writes of an incident when the Romans surrounded Jerusalem about 55 AD. A highly respected Jewish fighter named Eleazar often showed much boldness in the face of their enemy by being the last to leave a battle. In his last battle, he stayed outside the Jerusalem walls and talked with those on the walls. He was captured. The Roman general caused that he was stripped naked and placed where those in the city could see him. He was *"sorely whipped before their eyes."* Josephus further stated,

> *The city, with one voice, sorely lamented him, and the mourning proved greater than could well be supposed, upon the calamity of a single person*[41]

The Roman general recognized this and commanded that a cross be posted before the city as if they were going to crucify Eleazar. The city was horrified by this prospect. Eleazar convinced the city to save themselves and him from this "most pitiable of deaths" by giving themselves up to the Romans. The people feared crucifixion.

Zias made note of an important understanding that relates to attaching victims to the Patibulum. He wrote,

> *Eyewitness accounts by prisoners of war in Dachau during WWII reported that victims suspended from beams by their wrist, which were tied, expired within ten minutes if their feet were weighted or tied down and within one hour if their feet were unweighted and the victim was able to raise and lower himself to permit respiration. Death in this manner, which is one form of crucifixion, was the result of suffocation.*[42]

Normally we think of someone being attached to the patibulum so that the body and their arms formed a "T" shape. But careful analysis shows that this was not always the case. Let us consider the two thieves who were crucified at the same time as the Savior. They were nailed to their crosses on the morning at the same time as the Savior.

---

[41] Whiston, Josephus Complete Works, 596 (Wars, book VII, Ch VI, P 4)
[42] "Crucifixion in Antiquity" :P. 6-7

Late in the afternoon the soldiers broke their legs. This breaking of their legs was to hasten their deaths. Dying on the Sabbath day could create Jewish heated complaints, which could cause Jewish fighters to respond. The Romans did not want to incite this discontent. Their deaths occurred shortly following the breaking of their legs and prior to dusk, the beginning of the Sabbath.

They would die in a short time, if their hands were attached to the patibulum, so that their arms were near the vertical and not the horizontal "T" shape. With arms near the vertical and broken legs their deaths would occur in a very short time, just like the Dachau prisoners.

The Savior was attached to the patibulum just like the two thieves. His arms were near vertical to the patibulum. The record makes no mention of his legs being broken. He was already dead.

GETHSEMANE

The Savior's experience in Gethsemane is critical to understanding his atonement and his bitter cup experience.

Many feel that they know and understand his Gethsemane suffering. Many feel that he suffered directly from the sins of all mankind. However, if one will look at the Savior's revelations carefully, a different understanding can be identified from what is commonly understood. To get a correct knowledge of his Gethsemane suffering, it depends on understanding the Savior's words.

The Savior said of his suffering in the Garden,

> *For behold, **I, God, have suffered these things for all**, that they might not suffer if they would repent;*
>
> *But if they would not repent they must suffer even as I*
>
> *Which suffering caused myself, even God, the greatest of all, to tremble because of pain, and to bleed at every pore, and to suffer both body and spirit—and would that I might not drink the bitter cup, and shrink*[43]

---

[43] D&C 19:16-18

His bleeding at every pore only happened in his Garden experience. The expression that is important to be addressed at this time, is that he "*suffered these things for all*."

Definition of These Things

The expression "these things" appears numerous times in the scriptures. The count is,

- ➢ 201 in the New Testament,
- ➢ 117 in the Doctrine & Covenants,
- ➢ 366 in the Book of Mormon.

There is not a single definition for the expression these things in all of these usages. In each case, the meaning of the expression depends on the context in which the expression is used. The following are examples showing how the definition of the expression *these things* is determined.

In writing of his father preaching to the Jewish population, Nephi stated,

> *And it came to pass that the Jews did mock him because of the things which he testified of them; <u>for he truly testified of their wickedness and their abominations; and he testified that the things which he saw and heard, and also the things which he read in the book, manifested plainly of the coming of a Messiah, and also the redemption of the world.</u>*
>
> *And when* **the Jews heard <u>these things</u> they were angry with him;** *yea, even as with the prophets of old, whom they had cast out, and stoned, and slain; and they also sought his life, that they might take it away.*[44]

In this quote these things refer to the condemnations, warnings and truths that Lehi preached. Then the term "these things" is used in place of repeating the things (which are many) contained in the first paragraph.

After Laban rejected the request for the brass plates, Nephi and his brothers returned to their vacated home to get their treasures which

---

[44] 1 Nephi 1:19-20

had been left behind. These treasures were to be offered to Laban for the brass plates,

> And it came to pass that we went down to the land of our inheritance, and we did gather together our gold, and our silver, and our precious things.
>
> And after we had gathered **these things** together, we went up again unto the house of Laban.[45]

Here the term *these things* refers to the gold, silver and their precious things they collected from their vacated home.

From the Doctrine and Covenants, the Lord told Hyrum,

> Deny not the spirit of revelation, nor the spirit of prophecy, for wo unto him that denieth **these things**[46]

Joseph received this revelation from the Savior and are the Savior's words as he provided them in our English language. Here the term *these things* is used to refer to the things previously stated which are the spirit of revelation and the spirit of prophecy.

The expression "these things" is used to refer to something that was expressed prior to the usage of the term. It is used to refer to the things previously written so that those things would not have to be rewritten to identify them.

Suffering These Things
The Savior stated,

> For behold, I, God, have suffered **these things** for all, that they might not suffer if they would repent;[47]

The expression 'these things" refers to something written prior to this usage. We need to look at the preceding language in the revelation (Section 19) itself. A casual reading of the previous verses in Section 19, does not provide a quick answer about the meaning of *these things*. As with other concepts, we need to study the preceding language carefully to understand it's meaning.

---

[45] 1 Nephi 3:22-23
[46] D&C 11:23-25
[47] D&C 19:16

This revelation was a call to repentance for Martin Harris and deals with God's decreed judgments and punishments of humankind. The verses that are applicable to understanding *these things* he suffered are:

> *And surely **every man must repent or suffer, for I, God, am endless***
>
> *Wherefore, I revoke not the **judgments** which I shall pass, but **woes shall go forth, weeping, wailing and gnashing of teeth, yea, to those who are found on my left hand.***
>
> *Nevertheless, it is not written that there shall be no end to **this torment**,* [48]

These are the only preceding verses which refer to sufferings, judgments, woes and torment which might explain the source of the Savior's suffering. The key expression to this discussion from this quote is,

> *every man must repent or suffer*

The statement is clear. Every man MUST REPENT OR SUFFER. No single person is excluded. This suffering is described as *"woes shall go forth, weeping, wailing and gnashing of teeth."* This describes the wicked who are subject to Satan. Alma recorded this to his son, Corianton,

> *And then shall it come to pass, that the spirits of the wicked, yea, who are evil—for behold, they have no part nor portion of the Spirit of the Lord; for behold, they chose evil works rather than good; therefore the spirit of the devil did enter into them, and take possession of their house—and **these shall be cast out into outer darkness; there shall be weeping, and wailing, and gnashing of teeth, and this because of their own iniquity, being led captive by the will of the devil.***
>
> *Now this is the state of the souls of the wicked, yea, in darkness, and a state of awful, fearful looking for the fiery indignation of the wrath of God upon them; thus they remain in this state, as*

---

[48] D&C 19:4-6

well as the righteous in paradise, until the time of their resurrection.[49]

It should be noted that the wicked remain in this state until the time of their resurrection.

Mosiah recorded,

> *then shall the **wicked be cast out, and they shall have cause to howl, and weep, and wail, and gnash their teeth;** and this because they would not hearken unto the voice of the Lord*
>
> ***For they are carnal and devilish, and the devil has power over them***;[50]

Satan himself reacts in this same manner. After seeing the Savior, Moses was visited by Satan and a conversation ensued. During this conversation, Satan wanted Moses to worship him but when Moses refused, Satan ranted and Moses feared and saw the bitterness of hell.[51] Then Satan,

> ***cried with a loud voice, with weeping, and wailing, and gnashing of teeth;*** *and he departed hence, even from the presence of Moses*[52]

The unrepentant will suffer from Satan in hell. This discussion shows that the Savior suffered directly from Satan in the Garden. The Savior stated this by his own words. He,

> *suffered these things for all*
> *But, if they would not repent they must suffer even as I;*[53]

Christ suffered directly from Satan in the Garden and the unrepentant will suffer from Satan in hell even as the Savior suffered from Satan in the Garden. Christ suffered in the same way that Joseph Smith started to suffered from Satan,

> ***I had scarcely done so, when immediately I was seized upon by some power which entirely overcame me, and had such an***

---

[49] Alma 40:13-14
[50] Mosiah 16:2-3
[51] Moses 1:19-20
[52] Moses 1:22
[53] D&C 19:16-17

astonishing influence over me as to bind my tongue so that I could not speak. Thick darkness gathered around me, and it seemed to me for a time as if I were doomed to sudden destruction.

But, exerting all my powers to call upon God to deliver me out of the power of this enemy which had seized upon me, and **at the very moment when I was ready to sink into despair and abandon myself to destruction—not to an imaginary ruin, but to the power of some actual being from the unseen world, who had such marvelous power as I had never before felt.* [54]

This suffering was so strong and painful as to cause the Savior to bleed at every pore. One other thing needs to be stated and emphasized. This entire discussion about *these things* is from Section 19. At the very beginning of this section the Savior states:

I am Alpha and Omega, Christ the Lord; yea, even I am he, the beginning and the end, the Redeemer of the world.

I, having accomplished and finished the will of him whose I am, even the Father, concerning me—having done this that I might subdue all things unto myself—

Retaining all power, even to the destroying of Satan and his works at the end of the world, and the last great day of judgment, *which I shall pass upon the inhabitants thereof, judging every man according to his works and the deeds which he hath done.*[55]

In these verses the Savior strongly confirms that he is the Savior and has,

all power, even to the destroying of Satan and his works at the end of the world

Even though the Savior tells us that he subjected himself to Satan in the Garden, he has the power and will destroy Satan and his works at the end of the world. His subjection to Satan was temporary and only lasted in the Garden.

---

[54] Smith, History of the Church 1:15–16
[55] D&C 19:1-3

Father's Presence

In order for us to return to the presence of God, we must conform to special requirements to live in his presence. The Savior also had to conform to these requirements. Joseph describes the environment in which God dwells:

> ***Some shall rise to the everlasting burnings of God; for God dwells in everlasting burnings***[56]

Joseph Smith gave a sermon on Sunday May 12, 1844 that explains additional requirements to be in the presence of God. On that date Thomas Bullock recorded the Prophet as saying,

> <u>God Almighty himself dwells in eternal fire</u>; **flesh and blood cannot go there, for all corruption** [bodies with blood] ***is devoured by the fire. Our God is a consuming fire.*** –<u>when our flesh is quickened by the spirit, there will be no blood in the tabernacles</u>[57]

The Savior had to eliminate all of his blood from his body. King Benjamin stated that the Savior bled from **every pore** of his body.[58]

Luke describes the Savior as sweating **great drops of blood** and places this event in the Garden of Gethsemane.[59]

The Savior gave his own statement of his bleeding, He said

> *Which suffering caused myself, even God, the greatest of all, to tremble because of pain, and* **to <u>bleed at every pore</u>**, *and to suffer both body and spirit—and would that I might not drink the bitter cup, and shrink.* [60]

To bleed at every pore of a body means that he bled profusely.

Becoming Immortal

George Laub[61] recorded Joseph's May 12, 1844 address as,

---

[56] Smith, History of The Church, vol 6, P 317
[57] Smith, History of the Church, 6, P 366 (Spoken on 10 May 1844)
[58] Mosiah 3:7
[59] Luke 22:44
[60] D&C 19:16-18
[61] If needed, Reread the Section "George Laub Recording"

*Concerning Resurrection Flesh and Blood cannot inherit the kingdom of god or the kingdom that god inherits or inhabits. But **the flesh without the blood and the Spirit of god flowing in the vains in Sted of blood** for blood is the part of the body that causes corruption.* <u>*therefore we must be changed in the twinkle of an Eye or have to lay down these tabernacles and leave the blood vanish away*</u>*. Therefore,* **Jesus Christ left his blood to atone for the Sins of the world that he might ascend into the present(ce) of the Father.**[62]

The last sentence is the important one. It shows that the Savior left all of his blood to return to the presence of the Father. In the Garden all of his blood was bled out, so he could return to the presence of the Father.

When the Savior was born, he had blood flowing through his veins from his mother and spirit in his veins from his Father. When in the garden, the Savior shed all of the blood out of his body leaving only spirit in his veins. This made him immortal so he could return to the presence of the father.

There are about 6 pints of blood in an ordinary person. The amount of blood in the Savior's body would be about half of that. The other half was spirit from his father. That would require about 3 pints of blood to be eliminated from the Savior's body to become immortal.

The proportion of his spirit fluid to blood was constantly changing in his body as he was bleeding. The fluid spirit would become more dominant in his body as the blood left. When the blood was gone, all that was left was spirit flowing through his veins and he was immortal.

The significance of this discussion is that it demonstrates that the Savior became immortal from his Garden experience. He was immortal when he suffered his scourging, the soldier's maltreatments, the crown of thorns and his cross endurance.

The Savior said he had the power to lay down his life and to take it again,[63] Having this power he died on the cross, when his spirit body left his physical body. Following his ministering in the world of spirits, he exercised his power and his spirit body entered into his

---

[62] Ehat, Words of Joseph Smith, P 370-371 (Spoken on 10 May 1844)
[63] John 10:17-18

physical body in an immortal state. This was his resurrection! His spirit body reinhabited his physical body and there was no blood in his body. He was immortal!

Right after his resurrection he told Mary,

> *Touch me not; for I am not yet ascended to my Father: but go to my brethren, and say unto them, I ascend unto my **Father, and your Father; and to my God, and your God.***[64]

He was immortal with no blood in his body and could return to the Father's presence.

Spear and Blood

It is recorded that following his death, a soldier pierced the side of the Savior and *blood and water* came from the wound.[65]

This author could find no plausible natural explanation for water to flow from the side of the Savior. This water was "spirit" that was flowing through the veins of the savior. It is probably the closest word that could be used to describe *"spirit."*

The word blood was probably added by a scribe not understanding that there was no blood in the veins of the Savior. According to his understanding blood had to be there but the word water was left in the record which gives us the clue to what spirit is like.

Personal Sins

This discussion shows that in the Garden, the Savior suffered at the hands of Satan for all humankind and became immortal. The Savior completed his atonement following which the Father made him our judge.

It is important to note that if he had not suffered as described above, then as Jacob stated, we would become subject to Satan throughout eternity because no infinite atonement would have been provided.[66] The Savior could have withdrawn anytime from the atonement events, but he was true to his commitment to the Father.

---

[64] John 20:17
[65] John 19:34
[66] 2 Nephi 9:8-9

He did not take upon him our individual personal sins or suffer for them in the Garden! In the Garden he did not suffer for Joe Doe's adultery or Jane Doe's theft. The Savior said,

And surely every man must repent or suffer[67]

If Joe Doe and Jane Doe do not repent, then they will suffer what the Savior suffered, which is suffering in hell at the hand of Satan. If there is no repentance there is suffering.

The Savior does not take upon him our personal sins without first accepting our repentance. No repentance, no forgiveness! When a person repents and is baptized, they receive the Holy Ghost and they are forgiven by the Savior. This forgiveness is the first time when the Savior takes upon him our individual personal sins. He makes his atonement personal for us with this forgiveness!

His Greater Suffering

There is one difference between mortals suffering from Satan and what the Savior suffered. That difference is that Christ suffered these things while in the flesh. The Savior said,

Which suffering caused myself, even God, the greatest of all, **to tremble because of pain, and to bleed at every pore** *and to suffer,* **both body and spirit**[68]

The Savior had both body and spirit pain. There is no way to measure or fully understand this combination of pain except to understand that it was extremely intense and probably beyond the capability of mortals to endure. All wicked mortal people will die before they are cast into hell. They will not suffer physical pain.

MALTREATMENTS

Immediately following his Garden ordeal, he was arrested and his maltreatments began. These trials challenged his willpower, his love and commitment to the Father and to us as his brothers and sisters. These were tests initiated by others that would determine whether he would remain sinless and fulfill his atonement or that he might fail and no atonement made.

---

[67] D&C 19:4
[68] D&C 19:18

Being Immortal - Suffering Pain

If the Savior's body was immortal, did that alter his suffering physical pain? By his own admission he has stated that he suffered great pain.[69]

He suffered pain because of the physical abuse of the guards, the scourging and wounds from the nails pinning him to the cross. We need to recognize that pain in any body is generated by the disturbance of nerve cells, which are part of the nervous system. The Savior's nervous system is just like ours. The only difference between his body and our mortal bodies is the spirit flowing through his body.

Any time a guard would strike him with his fist, he would feel it just like we would. When they scourged him making his backside raw, he would feel the full intensity of pain just like we would. During his maltreatments, he suffered physical events that are not commonly understood. By examining the maltreatment events carefully, we can ascertain and describe the pains he really suffered.

Arrest, Trial and Maltreatments

These events were provocative. He was arrested, tried and found guilty of blasphemy by those who hated him. They were agents of Satan. The maltreatment events that followed his guilty verdict were Satan directed. They were intended to get the Savior to react and sin. If Satan could get the Savior to react to these maltreatments, Satan would win his battle because the Savior would not be sinless. He could not be our example and Savior.

Anger and retribution would be the most likely sins if the Savior had reacted to his maltreatment. Throughout his ministry, he had been faithful to his calling. We know that the Savior suffered grief beginning at the Garden and lasting to his death.[70] If he changed from that feeling of grief to something like retribution or anger, Satan would win by causing the Savior to sin. Humankind would lose for we would not have a sinless redeemer. But the Savior gave "no heed"[71] to these temptations.

---

[69] D&C 19:18
[70] Matthew 26:38, Mark 14:34
[71] D&C 20:22

These provocative maltreatments occurred following his arrest. First, he was taken to Annas[72] where the first maltreatment occurred. Annas and the people who were there knew what was going on and why the Savior was arrested. Annas asked Jesus about his disciples, and of his doctrine.[73] This was intended to see if the Savior would admit directly that he was the Son of God. The Savior did not respond directly to Annas but told him to ask those that heard him and that he taught no secrets. An officer did not like the way the Savior responded to Annas and struck him with the palm of his hand. Knowing that this was against Jewish law the Savior verbally challenged the officer saying,

> *If I have spoken evil, bear witness of the evil: but if well, why smitest thou me?*[74]

This is the only recorded response or complaint that the Savior made during the maltreatments he received. He silently endured the rest of all maltreatments.

Without any more discussion Annas sent the bound Savior to Caiaphas.[75] Since Judas had previously agreed to deliver the Savior to them, Caiaphas had assembled others so that a council could be convened as soon as the Savior arrived. The council was convened and witnesses called and nothing was found that could be used to condemn the Savior. Finally, Caiaphas asked the Savior whether he was the Son of God.

Matthew, Mark and Luke record the same answer given with some slight differences. All three recorded Caiaphas as saying that the Savior's answer was an admission that he was the Son of God. This was blasphemy. The council agreed and they declared that the Savior was worthy of death. It was very likely that this occurred around 10 pm and the maltreatments began. [Read DETERMINING PASSOVER EVENTS Page 180 for justification of this timing]

Matthew and Mark wrote that the maltreatments were delivered following the verdict. Luke records the maltreatments and then the verdict. John does not comment on the trial, verdict or the

---

[72] John 18:19-24
[73] John 18:19
[74] John 18:23
[75] Matthew 26:63-66, Mark 14:61-64, Luke 22:66-71

maltreatments. Probably, he felt that the gospels covered that topic well.

Luke records that the council verdict declaring the Savior was worthy of death was given "*as soon as it was day*"[76]. John records that the council took Jesus to Pilate "early" [77] on the same morning. Luke's record shows that the council was held at daylight and could not be accurate for several reasons. If the council met early and had witnesses, it would delay the meeting with Pilate which would make the meeting with Pilate more toward midday. That would make all the following events impossible to be completed at the times that are mentioned in other scriptures. Luke also records the maltreatments happening prior to the council trial. The maltreatments would not occur prior to his guilty verdict. Matthew and Mark's time accounts appear to be more accurate. In all probability the verdict was given well before midnight, which means that the maltreatments lasted for about 8-9 hours. [Read DETERMINING PASSOVER EVENTS page 180]

The maltreatments began as soon as the verdict was given. Luke records the maltreatments,

And the men that held Jesus mocked him, and smote him.

And when they had blindfolded him, they struck him on the face, and asked him, saying, Prophesy, who is it that smote thee?

And many other things blasphemously spake they against him.[78]

Nephi prophesied of these maltreatments when he recorded,

And the world, because of their iniquity, shall judge him to be a thing of naught; wherefore they scourge him, and he suffereth it; and they smite him, and he suffereth it. Yea, they spit upon him, and he suffereth it, because of his loving kindness and his long-suffering towards the children of men.[79]

It appears that it was not just one person who issued the maltreatments but each one coming forward, then another, taking

---

[76] Luke 22:66
[77] John 18:28
[78] Luke 22:64-65
[79] 1 Nephi 19:9

their turn to spit, mock, smote, (using their hand), buffet (using their fist) and ridicule him to break his will. They repeated these actions many times. Isaiah made this prophecy,

> *I gave my back to the smiters, and **my cheeks to them that plucked off the hair**: I hid not my face from shame and spitting.*[80]

This event surely happened, but was not recorded in the New Testament. Removing the hair from his face was an act to shame the Savior in the public view. But the worst was yet to come.

The council took the Savior to Pilate early in the morning who, after a short discussion, sent him to Herod. Herod questioned the Savior but got no answer. Herod and his men,

> *set him at naught, and mocked him, and arrayed him in a gorgeous robe, and sent him again to Pilate.*[81]

Pilate now had to deal with the council and their cry to crucify the Savior. The exchange between Pilate and the Jewish council and other assembled people is described in all four gospels.[82]

The next event that happened was the scourging. Luke records that an offer to scourge him was made but does not record that it happened. Matthew and Mark show that Pilate had him scourged. Then he was released to be crucified. The Savior felt the pain from this scourging just as we would feel it. Remember that some mortal men died while being scourged and that Josephus described those that were scourged as half dead.

He may have been scourged more harshly than mortals. There would be no blood showing on his back. The spirit that flowed through his body would show like water. Those making the strikes would probably continue longer with no blood showing. Following the scourging the Savior's back would be raw. The nerves were severely impacted giving a terrible, burning, highly intensified pain and would weaken the Savior significantly. His clothes were put back on, which intensified the back pain even more. Any person who has had a badly

---

[80] Isaiah 50:6
[81] Like 23:11
[82] Matthew 27:11-26, Mark 15:1-16, Luke 23:1-7, 13-25, John 19:1-16

sunburned back that has had cloth dragged across it, understands how that pain can intensify.

The soldiers took Jesus to the common hall called the Praetorium with all the soldiers present. Matthew then records this event,

> And they **stripped him**, and put on him a scarlet robe.
>
> And when they had platted a crown of thorns, they put it upon his head, and a reed in his right hand: and they bowed the knee before him, and mocked him, saying, Hail, King of the Jews!
>
> And **they spit upon him, and took the reed, and smote him on the head**.
>
> And after that they had mocked him, they took the robe off from him, and put his own raiment on him, and led him away to crucify him.[83]

The action of stripping him and putting on the scarlet robe would again cause him to feel the intensified back pain. The robe and the mocking were intended for humiliation. Picture the Savior sitting with the robe on, a crown of thorns and the reed as a mock scepter, and the soldiers kneeling in front of him and in mocking tones saying "Hail King of the Jews", and his back burning in pain. Then the soldiers rising and taking the reed to beat him about the head with the crown of thorns still there.

These soldiers were trained to inflict pain and humiliate their victims. A crown of thorns is not a customary torture instrument. Since he was the King of the Jews the soldiers created this crown of thorns to not only ridicule him but to cause him more pain. The pounding of the crown would drive the thorns into the skin and into the cranium. The attendant pain would be very sharp. Anyone who has had a syringe needle poke a bone or had a sharp pointed instrument pierce the skin and bone would understand how painful that can be. These thorns were not just touching the bones but were driven into the bone with the force from the reed. The soldiers would swing it hard to create as much pain as possible. The reed would be disintegrated when the act was completed but nevertheless it would drive some

---

[83] Matthew 27:28-31, Mark 15:16-20, John 19:1-3

thorns through the skin into the cranium. Even if the thorns were removed, the pain would continue.

Consider this scene. The Savior was being mocked. He had great powers. He was in a much-weakened condition enduring the events throughout the night from slapping, fists beatings, the physical scourging, mocking, robe changing and crown of thorns.

The fact that Simon was enlisted to carry the Savior's cross shows his weakened condition. The crown of thorns was causing intense pain at every thorn that pierced his scalp and especially those that pierced the bone. Yet, his self-control was firm. Silently he endured the mocking and maltreatments. As Nephi said he suffered it *"because of his loving kindness and his long-suffering towards the children of men."*[84]

John records that in this condition Pilate displayed him to the mob saying "Behold the man!" Pilate was hoping that the mob would agree to release the Savior. But the cries were to crucify him. Pilate offered to release the Savior according to a custom of the day but the crowd chanted to release Barabbas, a criminal, and to crucify the Savior. So, Pilate relented and released Barabbas and ordered the Savior to be crucified.[85]

It is not recorded whether the crown of thorns was removed prior to crucifixion. Some early Christian paintings show the Savior on the cross with the crown of thorns. It is likely that it was left on to continue as much pain and humiliation as possible as he was crucified. This would be compatible with the soldiers training. Public displaying this king with his prominent crown of thorns would add to the supposed humiliation of the Savior.

His Cross Pains

The first thing that would have happened after arriving at Golgotha would be nailing the Savior to the cross. It is likely that the cross was laying on the ground and the Savior laying on the cross while the nails were pegged. If the cross was standing erect, it would be a much more difficult task to support the Savior and nail him to the cross. After the nailing, the cross would have to be pulled to an erect

---

[84] 1 Nephi 19:9
[85] Luke 23;17-21

position with the pole inserted into a hole to support it upright. There would be a significant jarring to the Savior's body as the pole settled into the hole. This would cause a spike of pain to the Savior's body especially where the nails were pegged.

On the cross he had to contend with multiple pain and body issues. There would be the back pain from the scourging, pain from the nails supporting his body, pain from the thorny crown, thirst and fatigue from the punishing events.

It is unknown how the Savior's body reacted to the difficulty of breathing. Not being able to breathe properly probably would cause him some physical discomfort but not death. The closer to the vertical that the hands and wrists were nailed, the more difficulty in breathing would happen. He would have to push up with his feet to facilitate breathing causing more intense pain from the nails.

While this physical pain was increasing, the verbal abuse continued. Matthew wrote,

> *And they that passed by reviled him, wagging their heads,*
>
> *And saying, Thou that destroyest the temple, and buildest it in three days, save thyself. If thou be the Son of God, come down from the cross.*
>
> *Likewise also the chief priests mocking him, with the scribes and elders, said,*
>
> *He saved others; himself he cannot save. If he be the King of Israel, let him now come down from the cross, and we will believe him.*
>
> *He trusted in God; let him deliver him now, if he will have him: for he said, I am the Son of God.* [86]

This was the strongest maltreatment that could be mustered by Satan. The Savior's physical pain was at its most severe point and the verbal charges given were as biting as could be generated. However, the Savior gave no heed to their biting remarks.

---

[86] Matthew 27:39-43, Mark 15:29–32, Luke 23:39-43

Notice also that all the comments were that he should exercise his powers to preserve his life and that would show his powers to those who mocked him.

Nephi gives the true motivation of the Savior in conducting himself in the manner that he did,

> *And the world, because of their iniquity, shall judge him to be a thing of naught; wherefore they scourge him, and he suffereth it; and they smite him, and he suffereth it. Yea, they spit upon him, and he **suffereth it, because of his loving kindness and his long-suffering towards the children of men.*** [87]

All of these maltreatments and pains were designed by his persecutors to get the Savior to lose his self-control and react as the "natural man" would react. But the Savior never did respond as the natural man, knowing that all humankind would be lost to Satan, if he did. The Savior truly loved us by enduring what he did!

To illustrate the Savior's perfect self-control and love for us, remember the Roman soldiers who were men of war, were taught to make punishments cruel and painful as a deterrent to others. Remember that they were the ones who decided to provide the crown of thorns as a further humiliation of the Savior. They were not directed to do this but because they were taught to inflict as much pain as possible, they did it. In the final stages of his crucifixion as he hung on the cross, he demonstrated that there were no "natural man" characteristics in him for he said *"forgive them Father for they know not what they do"*[88]. The word "them" refers to the soldiers. This was a sincere genuine prayer given out of concern for the soldier's eternal welfare, who were unknowing in what they did.

We should note the soldier's reaction to the Savior's death. Matthew records,

> *Now when the centurion, and they that were with him, watching Jesus, saw the earthquake, and those things that were done, they feared greatly, saying,* **Truly this was the Son of God.** [89]

---

[87] 1 Nephi 19:9
[88] Luke 23:34, JST Luke 23:35
[89] Matthew 27:54, Mark 15:39, Luke 23:47

There is one last point that needs to be stressed and should be remembered. Though the Savior never succumbed to the maltreatments in keeping with his perfect character and his great love, he nevertheless suffered. One of the definitions of the word suffer is to "undergo or experience."[90]

This brings to mind the Savior's response to Joseph Smith's Liberty Jail prayer. The Lord in his response to that prayer describes the many trials that Joseph had already experienced and some that he could possibly face and then the Lord says,

> know thou, my son, that **all these things shall give thee experience**, and shall be for thy good.[91]

Then the Savior said his now famous statement,

> The Son of Man hath descended below them all.[92]

The Savior's experience or sufferings far exceeded that of Joseph's or Job's experience. The expression "them all" refers to any and all experiences suffered by man. Having that experience puts him in the position that the Father planned from the beginning. That Christ is to be our judge. These experiences gave the Savior the understanding where he could provide a "righteous" judgment. He would also know how to be merciful.

These experiences are sufficient for him to understand all trials that humankind faces. He can provide perfect mercy and give succor to help humankind so that at the final judgment he can provide the best possible kingdom and glory for all.

Cause of His Death

Death for the Savior was different than for mortal people. In his case death was the separation of his spirit from his body not the failure of some vital part of his body as happens to man.

Many writers have written and speculated about what caused the Savior to die. Failure of some body function is often identified.

---

[90] http://www.merriam-webster.com/dictionary/suffer. Last visited July 2016
[91] D&C 122:7
[92] D&C 122:8

A number of proposed causes of the death have been proposed. Such speculations are misplaced because he was immortal. These are proposed because the authors are looking for a mortal body failure causing his death.

Following Gethsemane, the Savior had only spirit running through his veins. At that time, his body could qualify to return to the presence of the Father because there was no blood left in his veins. However, he had to finish his atonement. He was required by the Father to be crucified[93] and he was nailed to the cross.

Decision to Die

Since Christ was commanded to give up his life by crucifixion,[94] The questions are "How long did he have to suffer on the cross before he chose to die? How would he know when he had completed the Father's command?" No scriptures clearly answer these questions.

However, there are two scriptures when analyzed together will help us understand the situation,

> *And about the ninth hour Jesus cried with a loud voice saying... My God, my God, why hast thou forsaken me?*[95]

James E. Talmage and Bruce R. McConkie confirmed this cry signified very great physical pain.[96]

John gives us the second scripture. The Savior arrived at the point of knowing his suffering was acceptable. It reads,

> *Jesus **knowing that all things were now accomplished** ... saith, I thirst ...*
> *When Jesus therefore had received the vinegar, he said, It is finished: and he bowed his head, and gave up the ghost.*[97]

---

[93] 3 Nephi 27:14
[94] John 10:16-17, 3 Nephi 27:13-16
[95] Matthew 27:46, JST Matthew 27:59, Mark 15:34-37
[96] Talmage, Jesus the Christ P 660-661; McConkie, The Mortal Messiah Vol 4, P 225
[97] John 19:28, 30

The meaning of "all things were now accomplished" is that the Savior knew his sacrifice and sufferings were acceptable to his Father and he could will his own death.

The Savior did not know at the time of his cry of pain that his suffering was acceptable to the Father. This is a critical understanding. If he knew that *"all things were now accomplished"* he would not be making his cry of pain to the Father. He would cause his spirit body to leave his physical body creating his death because he knew all was accomplished.

It is a very important concept to understand that when the Savior petitioned the Father with his cry of physical pain that he did not know whether his suffering was acceptable to the Father.

What the Savior was really communicating by his cry of physical pain was, "I am really hurting Father. It is difficult to bear this any longer. How much more do I need to suffer?"

The two scriptures above describe the Savior's last moments. They describe the same sequence of time. The time between the Savior's cry of pain and him knowing that *"all things were now accomplished"* was immediate.

Matthews recorded the Savior's last moment as,
> *Jesus, when he had cried again with a loud voice, yielded up the ghost.*[98]

Joseph Smith translated this verse to read,
> *Jesus, when he had cried again with a loud voice, saying, Father, it is finished, thy will is done and he yielded up the ghost.*[99]

This translated account by Joseph Smith also shows an immediate change from his cry of physical pain to knowing it was accepted. He then willed his death. Death was his spirit body leaving his physical body. The Savior's spirit body went to visit the world of spirits to finish the Father's command by ministering therein.

---

[98] Mathew 27:50
[99] Matthew 27:50, See Footnote

How did the Savior come to know that his suffering was acceptable to the Father? It seems obvious that the Father communicated to him that his suffering was sufficient.

It is important to understand that during the Savior's ministry the Father had communicated directly with the Savior. We do not have a record of these communications but we know they happened. In fact, the Father is the one who commanded the Savior to suffer on the cross. It was the Father who determined when his suffering was sufficient.

The elapsed time that the Savior suffered on the cross was some six or seven hours. Remember that he had been scourged prior to the cross. That scourging was probably extended because there was no blood showing. Remember also as he was on the cross, his pains would increase with time just like ours would increase. He would not die until he had confirmation from the Father that his suffering was acceptable and sufficient. It shows that the Savior suffered more intense pains and far longer than any mortal man.

This explains how the Savior is now able to judge us righteously. His pain was far greater than the pain of any mortal. His pain sufferings combined with his compassion and care for his siblings made him fully capable of make righteous judgments of us.

Final Moments

James E. Talmage places the time of nailing to the cross as occurring between 9am and 10am. He wrote,

> *Jesus was nailed to the cross during the forenoon of that fateful Friday,* **probably between nine and ten o'clock.** *At noon the light of the sun was obscured, and black darkness spread over the whole land. The terrifying gloom continued for a period of three hours,*[100]

The Savior finally arrived at his pain threshold. The scriptures state,

> *And about the ninth hour Jesus cried with a loud voice saying... My God, my God, why hast thou forsaken me?*[101]

---

[100] Talmage, Jesus the Christ P 660
[101] Matthew 27:46, JST Matthew 27:59, Mark 15:34-37

Up until this point the Savior had patiently endured all physical pain. This quoted statement made to the Father was definitely a cry of great physical pain. Of this event James E. Talmage wrote,

> At the **ninth hour, or about three in the afternoon**, *a loud voice, surpassing the most anguished **cry of physical suffering** issued from the central cross, rending the dreadful darkness. It was the voice of Christ: ... 'My God, my God, why hast thou forsaken me?' What mind of man can fathom the significance of that awful cry?* **It seems, that in addition to the fearful suffering incident to crucifixion, the agony of Gethsemane had recurred, intensified beyond human power to endure.** [102]

From Talmage we learn that the Savior was on the cross about six (6) hours before he willed his death. Any mortal person, who has suffered scourging and then crucifixion could not stay alive for this length of time. Many would die at the scourging but the Savior lasted for some 6 hours on the cross before he willed his death.

Talmage confirms that Christ's cry to the Father resulted from the great physical pain he was experiencing. Because of that intense pain, Talmage suggests that Christ re-suffered his Garden pains. He could not account for the pain intensity other than that.

Bruce R. McConkie also recognized this as a cry of great physical pain. He suggests that Christ re-suffered the pains of Gethsemane during the three (3) hours of darkness. He quoted James E. Talmage.[103] Both recognized the Savior's cry as a cry of great pain and couldn't account for the pain intensity other than suggesting that he re-suffered the pains of Gethsemane.

Re-Suffering Gethsemane?

Both Talmage and McConkie believe that Christ re-suffered his Garden sufferings while on the cross. He was suffering extreme pain as they had identified. This question of re-suffering the Garden pains needs to be addressed. When the Savior was in the Garden, he submitted himself to Satan's control experiencing his buffetings and control which caused him to feel physical and spiritual pain. This

---

[102] Talmage, Jesus the Christ P 660-661
[103] McConkie, The Mortal Messiah 4, P 225

suffering caused him to shed all of his blood out of his body making him immortal. There was no more blood in his body to bleed. He could not re-suffer what he had previously suffered.

Because of his immortality he was still alive but suffering from all that he had experienced starting with his Garden suffering. After feeling that he had fulfilled what the Father had commanded, his spirit body left his physical body. His spirit body went to direct affairs in the world of spirits.

State of His Body

The Savior's death occurred when the Savior willed his spirit body to leave his body. The Savior's relief from pain occurred when his spirit left the body. His physical body was immortal even though his spirit body was gone. His physical body would continue to function. Spirit was still flowing through his veins. It seems reasonable to believe that the Savior's body would not decay, but would begin to heal itself with spirit circulating through all of his body.

So, when the Savior re-inhabited his body, it was healed and he would have no pain.

BITTER CUP

When the Savior was alone in the Garden of Gethsemane, he prayed to his Father in Heaven. He petitioned the Father, if possible, to remove "*this cup from me*" but acknowledged that he would do the Father's will[104]. Following his resurrection, he appeared to the Nephites. One of his first statements was that he had "*drunk out of that bitter cup which the Father hath given me.*"[105]

The question is "what was the bitter cup that he suffered". From the Free Online Dictionary, the third definition of bitter reads,

> hard to bear; grievous; distressful:

Looking at the Savior's many life experiences, which ones fit the above description. When he was tempted directly by Satan to worship him, he was in complete control and suffered little if anything. There was nothing during his ministry that he experienced that fits this

---

[104] Matthew 26:39, 42, Mark 14:36, Luke 22:42
[105] 3 Nephi 11:10-12

description. His ministry was filled with teaching and ministering blessings to the people. The only period of his life where he began to experience events described as "hard to bear; grievous; distressful" was in the Garden. He described his suffering in the Garden,

> *Which suffering caused myself, even God, the greatest of all, to tremble because of pain, and to bleed at every pore, and to suffer both body and spirit—and would that I might not drink the bitter cup*[106]

He was arrested immediately following his Garden experience. At the arrest of the Savior, John records the following:

> *Then Simon Peter, having a sword drew it, and smote the high priest's servant, and cut off his right ear. The servant's name was Maldus.*
>
> *Then said Jesus unto Peter, put up thy sword into the sheath:* **the cup which my father has given me, shall I not drink it***?*

Peter had confirmed that he would defend the Savior with his life believing he would save Israel from the Romans. The Savior chastised Peter and confirmed that he had to experience the bitter cup. He was then arrested and endured the trial and maltreatments. He was finally crucified and died on the cross. When the Savior was on the cross, he said,

> *My God, my God, why hast thou forsaken me?*[107]

His pain and suffering could no longer be tolerated. Shortly following this plea, the Savior knew he had fulfilled all of the sufferings that he was commanded to do and he willed his death. His death was the final fulfillment of the Father's command.

So, we ask "What part of the Savior life caused him to experience events that are described as,

> *"hard to bear; grievous; distressful?"*

The only part of his life that fits this description is his suffering beginning with the Garden followed by the soldier maltreatments and

---

[106] D&C 19:18
[107] Matthew 27:46

ending with his being crucified. These three events are the bitter cup suffered by the Savior.

What was accomplished by this bitter cup?

- ➢ He suffered in the Garden from Satan and bled out to become immortal.
- ➢ He was tested with extreme physical maltreatments and remained sinless.
- ➢ He endured crucifixion and died on the cross to provide the resurrection for all humankind.

He suffered the bitter cup and fulfilled his atonement. He became our Savior and King.

SUFFERING PEOPLE PAINS?

There is a teaching that some have identified in the scriptures that needs to be addressed. That teaching is that the Savior will experience the "*pains and the illnesses of his people.*" Members have expressed that the Savior suffered "exactly" what we personally suffer and that he knows how to encourage and judge us because of that experience. In reality the Savior suffered far greater pain than any of us have suffered as he suffered during his bitter cup.

The most accurate scripture relating to this topic is what Alma said to the people of Gideon,

> And he shall go forth, **suffering pains and afflictions and temptations of every kind***; and **this that the word might be fulfilled which saith he will take upon him the pains and the illnesses of his people.***
>
> *And he will* **take upon him death**, *that he may loose the bands of death which bind his people; and he will take upon him **their infirmities**, that his bowels may be filled with mercy, according to the flesh, that he may know according to the flesh how to succor his people **according to their infirmities**.* [108]

The first paragraph addresses what the Savior personally suffered,

> *And he shall go forth,* **suffering pains and afflictions and temptations of every kind**

---

[108] Alma 7:11-12 see also D&C 18:11

This expression describes his bitter cup experience.

The second paragraph quoted above begins,

> And he will <u>take upon him</u> **death**,

This describes the final event of his bitter cup.

The Savior suffered in the Garden, then his maltreatments and finally on the cross, which sufferings constitute his bitter cup that he suffered. At the end of his bitter cup, he suffered death. There was no other part of his ministry during which he suffered pain, anguish, infirmities or inflictions. His bitter cup experience was the only time he suffered these things.

He did suffer temptations directly from Satan,[109] which he rejected but he suffered no pain during the experience.

His personal suffering was very intense because of his immortal state. If a mortal man had suffered the same events as the Savior, he would have died much earlier because a vital part of his mortal body would have failed causing his death. Being immortal, the Savior's life continued beyond the point that mortals could experience. His "bitter cup" experience gave him the understanding of,

> "*the pains and the illnesses of his people*"[110]

So, the Savior did not directly experience the pains and the sickness of his people. He experienced his own bitter cup experience that gave him that understanding. It was his entire bitter cup experience with the scourging, crown of thorns and death on the cross that gave him that experience. A careful search of the scriptures does NOT identify any other time or experiences that would give him this understanding.

During his bitter cup experience, he was judged and found guilty by the Jewish leadership. Barabbas, an accused murderer and robber, was released at the cry of the Jewish leadership instead of the Savior.

The Savior's experience on the cross was a prototype. He stood before high magistrates who pronounced judgments on him. He was found guilty and suffered their punishment. In like fashion the Savior became our judge and will judge us according to our works. The

---

[109] Luke 4:3-13
[110] Alma 7:11

following chart compares man's judgement of Christ and Christ's judgment of humankind.

Man's Judgment	Christ's Judgment
Jewish Leadership & Pilate were judges	Christ is the judge
Christ stood before man to be judged	Humankind will stand before Christ to be judged
Choice between two, Christ or Barabbas to be set free	Humankind separated into two groups, one having eternal life and one who will suffer. **A**
Barabbas who was guilty of breaking Jewish law was chosen to receive freedom	The righteous, will be free by inheriting the highest degree in the Celestial Kingdom
Christ was found guilty of breaking Jewish law and punished accordingly	Those found guilty of breaking God's law will suffer accordingly
Christ suffered scourging prior to his final punishment on the cross.	Some will be cast into hell to suffer the buffetings of Satan
Christ suffered unjustly	Christ's judgments will be just

A-Those who do not merit eternal life will suffer "Everlasting Fire". This suffering will conclude and a forgiveness given.

Emotion

Some writers have made the proposal that the Savior suffered severe emotional distress as part of his suffering.

The online Reference dictionary[111] defines emotion as,

> *1. an affective state of consciousness in <u>which</u> joy, sorrow, fear, hate, or the like, is experienced,* **as distinguished from cognitive and volitional states of consciousness.**
>
> *2.* **any of the feelings of** *joy, sorrow, fear, hate, love, etc.*

---

[111] http://dictionary.reference.com/browse/emotion?s=t. Last visited June 2020

3. any strong agitation of the feelings actuated by experiencing love, hate, fear, etc., and usually accompanied by certain physiological changes, as increased heartbeat or respiration, and often overt manifestation, as crying or shaking.

The key word in these definitions is feeling. An emotion is what you are currently feeling. Notice that the online Reference dictionary defines emotion as the "affective state of consciousness" as compared to the cognitive and volitional states of consciousness. The three states of consciousness of every person are defined as:

> Cognitive - pertains to those mental processes that use memory, judgment, perception and reasoning[112]
> Volitional - pertains to the power to exercise choice or the act of making a choice.[113]
> Affective – is our experiencing joy, sorrow, fear, hate or the like, which we call emotions.[114]

If we choose to study, our abilities in the cognitive area will increase especially in those areas we study. If we choose to watch movies, that can stir our emotions or feelings in various ways. Anger can affect our ability to make choices and our ability to exercise good judgment.

One Emotion

One important aspect of emotion is that only one emotion can be felt at any one time. When a person experiences an emotion, it is their current feeling. A person does not feel anger and love at the same time. A person may alternate between feelings but only one is felt at any one point in time. Some emotions are associated with each other. A person who is angry can become hateful. But not all people who experience anger are hateful people.

Nephi and his brothers, Laman and Lemuel, provide two examples showing how emotions change. Laman first approached Laban for the brass plates. Laban was angry and called Laman a robber and was going to slay Laman. He fled and joined his brothers. After discussing the situation, it was decided that they would go to their father's house and gather all of their valuables. These were to be

---

[112] https://www.dictionary.com/browse/cognitive?s=t, Last visited June 2020
[113] https://www.dictionary.com/browse/volitional, Last visited June 2020
[114] https://www.dictionary.com/browse/affective?s=t, Last visited June 2020

offered to Laban for the brass plates. Laban drove them out and they left their valuables behind as they fled for their lives. Then Laman and Lemuel were angry and beat Nephi and Sam with rods. An angel appeared, rebuking Laman and Lemuel and giving the group a charge to go back and get the brass plates and the Lord would deliver Laban into their hands.[115] After the angel left, Laman and Lemuel did not want to go back because of the following,

> *How is it possible that the Lord will deliver Laban into our hands? Behold, he is a mighty man, and he can command fifty, yea, even he can slay fifty; then why not us?*[116]

So Laman and Lemuel were feeling anger which subsided because of the angel. Then they were fearful at the thought that they needed to go back. They did not experience anger and fear at the same time.

On another occasion, Nephi and his brothers took a journey back to visit Ishmael and his family. The family agreed to join the group and travel to join Lehi. During the journey back, Laman and Lemuel and others rebelled and wanted to return to Jerusalem. Some wanted to return and others wanted to proceed.

Nephi chastised those who wanted to return, recounting that Jerusalem would be destroyed. He stated that the group would be preserved and given another land of promise to inhabit. Laman and Lemuel were angry with Nephi and bound him with cords. and planned to kill him. Nephi prayed to the Lord that he might break the cords. He was freed from the cords and he spoke to them again.

> *And it came to pass that **they were angry with me again**, and sought to lay hands upon me; but behold, one of the daughters of Ishmael, yea, and also her mother, and one of the sons of Ishmael, did plead with my brethren, insomuch that they did soften their hearts; and they did cease striving to take away my life.*

> *And it came to pass that **they were sorrowful, because of their wickedness**, insomuch that they did bow down before me, and did plead with me that I would forgive them of the thing that they had done against me.*

---

[115] 1 Nephi 3:25-31
[116] 1 Nephi 3:31

And it came to pass that I did frankly forgive them all that they had done," [117]

This quote illustrates that Nephi's brothers were angry because they still wanted to return to Jerusalem. They also objected to having Nephi lead the group, which the older brothers felt that it was their right. They wanted to lead the group. After the pleading of others in the group, their anger subsided. It was not until their anger was gone, that they could feel sorrow and asked for forgiveness from Nephi.

Two other examples are published in the Book of Mormon. There were two groups of people that left the land of Nephi's first inheritance and travelled to Zarahemla. One group was the people of King Limhi, who plotted their release from their Lamanite bondage and made their journey to Zarahemla.[118]

A second group was headed by Alma. Alma believed in Abinadi's message to king Noah and his court. He left the court and began teaching and baptizing the people. They avoided King Noah by fleeing from them and settling in a different area. but the group was later found by the Lamanites and forced into bondage. They plotted their escape and traveled to Zarahemla.[119]

After the arrival of Limhi and Alma's groups, King Mosiah received the records these groups possessed. He had these records read to his people.[120] Notice how King Mosiah's subjects fluctuated in their emotional responses after hearing these records read,

And now, when Mosiah had made an end of reading the records, his people who tarried in the land were struck with wonder and amazement.

For they knew not what to think; for when they beheld those that had been delivered out of bondage they were filled with exceedingly great joy.

---

[117] 1 Nephi 7:19-21
[118] Mosiah Ch. 22
[119] Mosiah Chap 18, 23-24
[120] Mosiah 25:5-6

> *And again, when they thought of their brethren who had been slain by the Lamanites they were filled with sorrow, and even shed many tears of sorrow.*
>
> *And again, when they thought of the immediate goodness of God, and his power in delivering Alma and his brethren out of the hands of the Lamanites and of bondage, they did raise their voices and give thanks to God.*
>
> *And again, when they thought upon the Lamanites, who were their brethren, of their sinful and polluted state, they were filled with pain and anguish for the welfare of their souls.*
>
> *And it came to pass that those who were the children of Amulon and his brethren, who had taken to wife the daughters of the Lamanites, were displeased with the conduct of their fathers, and they would no longer be called by the names of their fathers, therefore they took upon themselves the name of Nephi, that they might be called the children of Nephi and be numbered among those who were called Nephites.* [121]

The emotional reactions were *"wonder and amazement"*, *"sorrow"* to the point of tears, gratitude as expressed by *"giving thanks to God"*, *"pain and anguish"* and *"displeased."* Notice that these responses were related to their thoughts.

The Prophet Joseph Smith wrote an epistle from Liberty Jail on March 25, 1839 in which he wrote,

> *received some letters last evening-one from Emma, one from Don C. Smith, and one from Bishop Partridge-all breathing a kind and consoling spirit. We were much gratified with their contents. We had been a long time without information; and when we read those letters they were to our souls as the gentle air is refreshing,* **but our joy was mingled with grief, because of the sufferings of the poor and much injured Saints**. *And we need not say to you that <u>the floodgates of our hearts were lifted and our eyes were a fountain of tears</u>, but those who have not been enclosed in the walls of prison*

---

[121] Mosiah 25:11-12

> *without cause or provocation, can have but little idea how sweet the voice of a friend is.*[122]

In this quote, it appears that those in the jail were experiencing both joy and grief. The emotion that they were experiencing was joy as expressed by "*the floodgates of our hearts were lifted and our eyes were a fountain of tears.*" But Joseph and the others previously experienced heartfelt grief and concern for the suffering saints as they received reports of their exodus forced upon them.

When Joseph wrote of mingling grief with joy, he was exercising the "cognitive" functions and remembering the grief they had previously felt while feeling the joy of the letters. As he focused on those events, he might have felt that grief very briefly but temporarily. When returning to read the letters, he would feel joy. It is difficult to believe he was experiencing joy and deeply grieving for the injured saints at the same time. We can remember and talk about other emotions that we have experienced but not be feeling those same emotions at the moment.

Savior's Emotion

Did the Savior truly suffer emotional trauma or severe emotional trauma during his ordeal as some believe? What do we really know about the emotions that the Savior suffered through his atonement sufferings? When Christ was in the Garden, he took Peter, James and John with him a bit further than the others and prior to his prayer, he said,

> *My soul is exceeding **sorrowful, even unto death**: tarry ye here, and watch with me.*[123]

By his own words, he deeply felt this sorrow and he would suffer this until he died, for that sorrow was unto death. Being sorrowful is not experiencing severe emotional trauma as we might interpret this expression. When sorrow is felt deeply, we call it grief. The Savior is known as a man of sorrow and grief. Isaiah even prophesied of his grief,

---

[122] Smith, History of the Church, 3:294

[123] Matthew 26:38, Mark 14:34

> *He is despised and rejected of men; **a man of sorrows, and acquainted with grief***"[124]

There is no scriptural evidence that the Savior changed his sorrow to any other emotion. His statement indicates that he will experience this sorrow "unto death." The one event that needs explanation is his prayer on the cross to the Father about forgiving the soldiers. At the height of his pain and because of his perfect character, he recognized that the soldiers were not to be blamed for what he was experiencing. He understood that the soldiers were not acting on their own initiative. They were trained and ordered to conduct these maltreatments. It does show the Savior's great control in not giving way to anger or retribution against them but rather he asked that they be forgiven of their actions showing his great compassion for their eternal welfare, when he was suffering from severe pain.

The Savior visited the Nephites and foretold that the fourth generation of Nephites would fall into sin. He said,

> *But behold, **it sorroweth me** because of the fourth generation from this generation, for they are led away captive by him even as was the son of perdition; for they will sell me for silver and for gold,*[125]

While in heaven, many of us felt sorrow. In the revelation given to Joseph Smith and Sidney Rigdon they confirmed,

> *And this we saw also, and bear record, that an angel of God **who was in authority** in the presence of God, who rebelled against the Only Begotten Son whom the Father loved and who was in the bosom of the Father, was thrust down from the presence of God and the Son,*
>
> *And was called Perdition, for **the heavens wept over him**—he was Lucifer, a son of the morning.* [126]

When Satan fell from his station "in authority" we "wept" because our love for him had turned to sorrow over his failure.

---

[124] Isaiah 53:3

[125] 3 Nephi 27:32

[126] D&C 76:25-26

When the Savior granted the three Nephites their desire that they remain on earth to continue their mission, they became changed and not subject to mortal frailties. The Savior said this to them,

> *And again, ye shall not have pain while ye shall dwell in the flesh, **neither sorrow save it be for the sins of the world;** and all this will I do because of the thing which ye have desired of me, for ye have desired that ye might bring the souls of men unto me, while the world shall stand*[127]

If the Savior was suffering sorrow throughout his ordeal, he could not have suffered severe emotional trauma or severe mental distress as some believe.

Humankind has experienced some things the Savior has not experienced. These are sinful thoughts and actions. Obviously if he had experienced these things, he would not have been a perfect example.

Suffering Alone

One of the things that people suffer is the challenge of being afflicted in some way and being alone to endure it. Older people, after losing a spouse, deeply feel this loneliness. The Savior suffered this more deeply than any mortal man.

When all is finished, the Savior will present the Father with the kingdom,

> *When he shall deliver up the kingdom, and present it unto the Father, spotless, saying: I have overcome and **have trodden the wine-press alone**, even the wine-press of the fierceness of the wrath of Almighty God.* [128]

From this scripture, we see that the winepress is symbolic of the "fierceness of the wrath of almighty God" or the fiercest requirement ever given of God. The wine-press represents the sufferings in the Garden of Gethsemane, the soldier's maltreatments and on the cross, i.e. his bitter cup. He suffered these things alone.

---

[127] 3 Nephi 28:9
[128] D&C 76:107

It is true that an angel appeared to the Savior strengthening him.[129] This strengthening undoubtedly reminded him of the importance that all humankind was dependent upon his fulfilling the atonement. Because of his love for the Father and his siblings, the Savior did not withdraw. The angel left after his encouragement and the Savior suffered all that he did alone.

---

[129] Luke 22:43

■SALVATION OF MORTALS■

Our earth is not the first earth which our Father has created,

> *And the Lord God spake unto Moses, saying: The heavens, they are many, and they cannot be numbered unto man; but they are numbered unto me, for they are mine.*
>
> <u>*And as one earth shall pass away, and the heavens thereof even so shall another come; and there is no end to my works, neither to my words.*</u>
>
> *For behold,* **this is my work and my glory—to bring to pass the immortality and eternal life of man.** [130]

Our Father wants his children to become immortal and to have eternal life with him. Everyone, who has lived on this earth, will become immortal. The atonement provided by the Savior makes this happen. But he knows that some children will not qualify for eternal life. Nevertheless, that is his goal!

The atonement of our Savior provides that all will be resurrected and become immortal regardless of their conduct. The options as to where our Father's children will be consigned in eternity are,

- ➢ Celestial Kingdom
  - Highest Degree – eternal life [131]
  - Second Degree and Third Degree [132]
- ➢ Terrestrial Kingdom [133]
- ➢ Telestial Kingdom [134]
- ➢ Outer Darkness [135]

To qualify for "eternal life" is dependent on the decisions each of us makes as we journey through life.

---

[130] Moses 1:37-39
[131] D&C 76:50-70
[132] D&C 131:1-4
[133] D&C 76:71-80
[134] D&C 76:81-89
[135] D&C 76:25-38

BAPTISM

No one is born into the Savior's Church. All must be baptized to join his Church except children under age 8 years. The Savior stated this concerning those who are received into the Church of Jesus Christ of Latter-Day Saints by baptism,

> *All those who humble themselves before God, and desire to be baptized, and come forth with broken hearts and contrite spirits, and witness before the church that they have truly **repented of all their sins, and are willing to take upon them the name of Jesus Christ, having a determination to serve him to the end,** and truly manifest by their works that they have received of the Spirit of Christ unto the remission of their sins, shall be received by baptism into his church.*[136]

Children of members are normally baptized when they turn eight years of age. This is done that they may have the Holy Ghost to be with them and help them to be faithful to the Savior. Of course, they have to accept the teachings of the Savior as they grow up.

FORGIVENESS

When a person is baptized with humility and sincerity, they are forgiven of their sins. The Savior told Alma prior to the Savior's birth,

> *For behold, this is my church; whosoever is baptized shall be baptized unto repentance. And whomsoever ye receive shall believe in my name; and **him will I freely forgive.*** [137]

Lord also said,

> *Behold, he who has repented of his sins, the same is forgiven, and **I, the Lord, remember them no more.***[138]

If we continue faithfully to find out about the Savior and follow his teaching, we will be identified as guiltless to the Father at the final

---

[136] D&C 20:37
[137] Mosiah 26:22 See also D&C 29:26-29
[138] D&C 58:42

judgment. To be held guiltless means that we will be able to return to his presence,

> *if he endureth to the end, behold, him will I hold guiltless before my Father at that day when I shall stand to judge the world.* [139]

Maintaining Forgiveness

However, forgiveness is a conditional event until the death of an individual. The Savior said,

> *And now, verily I say unto you, I, the Lord, will not lay any sin to your charge; go your ways and sin no more;* **but unto that soul who sinneth shall the former sins return**, *saith the Lord your God.* [140]

After repentance and knowingly committing sin, those former sins are then remembered by the Savior. In the Kirtland temple dedicatory prayer, Joseph pleaded on behalf of all members of the Church,

> *Jehovah, have mercy upon this people, and as all men sin forgive the transgressions of thy people, and* **let them be blotted out forever.** [141]

To be "blotted out" refers to this concept that the Savior will remember them no more. Alma gave the most descriptive verse in the Book of Mormon about how the Savior provides forgiveness for individual sins,

> *Now the Spirit knoweth all things; nevertheless the Son of God suffereth according to the flesh that he might take upon him the sins of his people,* **that he might blot out their transgressions according to the power of his deliverance**; *and now behold, this is the testimony which is in me.* [142]

Even those who are active members need to be careful about their activity and attitudes. The Lord said of those who are slothful,

---

[139] 3 Nephi 27:16
[140] D&C 82:7
[141] D&C 109:34
[142] Alma 7:13

> *Wherefore, now let every man learn his duty, and to act in the office in which he is appointed, in all diligence.*
>
> **He that is slothful shall not be counted worthy to stand, and he that learns not his duty and shows himself not approved shall not be counted worthy to stand.**[143]

Those who learn not their duty would include the lazy and would include those who focus on the things of the world to the exclusion of exercising faith in the Savior. Other activities may not be sinful, but those who engage in them to the exclusion of active works of righteousness are at high risk. The Lord further said,

> *For behold, it is not meet that I should command in all things; for he that is compelled in all things, the same is a slothful and not a wise servant;* **wherefore he receiveth no reward.**
>
> *But he that doeth not anything until he is commanded, and receiveth a commandment with doubtful heart, and keepeth it with slothfulness,* **the same is damned.**[144]

Our Negative or hesitant attitude about being active in our Church and worshiping the Savior, can prevent us from qualifying for eternal life. To be damned is to be not worthy of eternal life. Joseph Smith wrote,

> *It is impossible for a man to be saved in ignorance.* [145]

We must be diligent in learning about the Savior and his teachings. Those who are identified as receiving "*no reward*" or "*damned*" are those who will not inherit eternal life. To maintain our forgiveness, we continue to serve by following the Savior and his commandments, whenever and however we can to the end of our mortal lives.

Perfection and Sin

There is a common notion in the Church that as Church members we continue to sin even up to our death because we are not perfect. Perfection is that elusive status that we can never reach in mortality. We equate non-perfection with sin, but perfection includes learning

---

[143] D&C 107:99-100, D&C 58:26
[144] D&C 58:26- 29
[145] D&C 131:6

eternal principles that relate to righteously functioning in mortality and in eternity. This process extends well beyond the grave. Each of us will be at a different level in learning of these eternal principles, when we die.

Working and laboring in the kingdom of God has a positive effect on our relationship with the Savior and our Heavenly Father. There are two scriptures in the New Testament that shed light on this concept,

> *Brethren, if any of you do err from the truth, and one convert him;*
>
> *Let him know, that he which converteth the sinner from the error of his way shall save a soul from death, and shall hide a multitude of sins.* [146]

And,

> *And above all things have fervent charity among yourselves: for charity shall cover the multitude of sins.* [147]

A person who is influential in the conversion of another person is one who furthers the Lord's work. That is, they are sharing the gospel with others as the Lord has commanded us.

A person who develops true charity is one whose conduct in this life is showing concern and support in various ways for others especially for those in distress. This shows that we are trying to follow the Savior and will be recognized by the Savior.

In connection with this concept, the Savior exercised mercy in giving forgiveness to some elders in Kirtland. Some of these elders had sinned and probably had not fully repented but all were taking active steps to prepare for and fulfill a commandment to travel to Zion (Missouri). This was not a simple task and was taking weeks to prepare. Of these the Lord said,

> *For verily I say unto you, I will that ye should overcome the world; wherefore I will have compassion upon you.*

---

[146] James 5:19-20
[147] 1 Peter 4:8

> *There are those among you who have sinned; but verily I say, for this once, for mine own glory, and for the salvation of souls,* ***I have forgiven you your sins***.
>
> *I will be merciful unto you, for I have given unto you the kingdom.* [148]

The Lord in exercising his judgment powers was willing to give them forgiveness for their dedicated activity of preparing to travel to Missouri as the Prophet Joseph Smith was directing. This seems to demonstrate that we are progressing in the character traits needed to become like our Savior when we are actively pursuing and implementing activities which further the work of the Savior. As we evaluate our own conduct to ensure that it complies with the Savior's commandments, we have less propensity to sin.

We are not perfect, but our dedicated efforts to be like the Savior, will be acceptable to him.

With regard to gaining further light and truth. Joseph Smith wrote,

> *Whatever* ***principle of intelligence we attain unto in this life, it will rise with us in the resurrection.***
>
> *And if a person gains more knowledge and intelligence in this life through his diligence and obedience than another, he will have so much the advantage in the world to come.* [149]

Intelligence is light and truth.[150] The Lord explained in the revelations Joseph received,

> *And no man receiveth a fulness unless he keepeth his commandments.*
>
> ***He that keepeth his commandments receiveth truth and light, until he is glorified in truth and knoweth all things***.[151]

Further,

> *The glory of God is intelligence, or, in other words, light and truth.*

---

[148] D&C 64:2-4
[149] D&C 130:18-19
[150] D&C 93:29
[151] D&C 93:27-28

> *Light and truth forsake that evil one.* [152]

Our goal in this mortality should be to gain as much knowledge, light, truth and good works as we are able.

INFINITE ATONEMENT

Whether one uses the expression "infinite atonement" or "resurrection", the meaning is the same. The resurrection which is provided by the Savior's atonement means that a body will be provided for every individual who has lived on this earth. That body will be the same stature as the body that died. Most people who hear or read of the "infinite atonement" think of a mature adult. Babies and children, who have died in their youth, will be resurrected.

Jacob, Nephi's brother, is the first person in the Book of Mormon to use the expression "*infinite atonement.*" He also talked of the words "corruption" and "incorruption". The word "*corruption*" when used in the scriptures refers to our mortal bodies being subject to death and when our bodies "*put on incorruption*" they are resurrected and live forever.

MARRIAGE COVENANT

It is extremely important for each of us who have access to a temple to be married by an authorized representative in the temple. If we do not do this, we will NOT have our marriage partner with us in the Celestial Kingdom. Joseph Smith recorded this revelation in his diary and history in Nauvoo, Illinois, July 12[th,] 1843. The title to this revelation was approved by Joseph Smith and recorded as,

> *Revelation on the Eternity of the Marriage Covenant Including Plurality of Wives.*[153]

This revelation is Section 132 in the current version of the Doctrine and Covenants. According to the wording, this revelation is about the "*eternity of the marriage covenant.*" There are consequences if the proper steps are not taken to be married properly in the temple. Joseph records the following at the beginning of the revelation:

> *For behold, I reveal unto you* ***a new and an everlasting covenant****; and if ye abide not that covenant, then are ye damned;*

---

[152] D&C 93:36-37

[153] Smith, History of the Church 5:501

for no one can reject this covenant and be permitted to enter into my glory.[154]

If this is not done, the couple though civilly married will not "*be permitted to enter into my glory.*" This temple marriage covenant is required to be completed by married couples to have eternal life. Eternal life is life with the Father and the Savior throughout eternity. The expression bolded above which is "*a new and an everlasting covenant*" identifies the marriage covenant. This exact expression is found in only one other place in the scriptures. That is in section 22 verse one.

Two key words in this initial expression are "a" and "an." These words are singular in form. This covenant is "a new covenant" and it is "an everlasting covenant." It is a single covenant which is new and everlasting and not multiple covenants.

This marriage ceremony is performed in the temple by a person authorized to perform such marriages. The word "new" has meaning because it is new to both participants every time it is performed. Once it is performed it is never repeated for the same two participants. As quoted above, this covenant is the only one recognized by Our Father in Heaven in eternity. He explains that if we reject this covenant, we cannot be in his presence in eternity. In other words, we are not qualified for eternal life.

The expression "*a new and an everlasting covenant*" is never repeated but is shortened to "*new and everlasting covenant*" in following paragraphs. When the expression "new and everlasting covenant" is used in the scriptures, it refers to this marriage covenant. Sometimes it is referred to as the everlasting covenant or new covenant.

The Covenant

In the above quote we are told not to reject this covenant. If it is rejected, we cannot enter into the presence of the Father or his son. Rejection of this covenant is that a couple marries but does not prepare themselves to go to the temple and be properly married for

---

[154] D&C 132:4

"*time and all eternity.*" Another way to reject this covenant is to commit serious sin following a proper temple marriage

Verse 7 - The law governing this covenant is,

> *the conditions of **this law** are these: <u>All covenants, contracts, bonds, obligations, oaths, vows, performances, connections, associations, or expectations,</u> that are not made and entered into and **sealed by the Holy Spirit of promise, of him who is anointed**...*
>
> *are of no efficacy, virtue, or force in and after the resurrection from the dead; for **all contracts that are not made unto this end have an end when men are dead.*** [155]

This list of words describes potential relationships, feelings and expectations that may exist between people. It does not refer to ordinances. The list of words is

- Covenants   between people
- Contracts   between people
- Bonds   between people
- Obligations   between people
- Oaths   between people or individually
- Vows   between people
- Performances   between people
- Ceremonies   between people
- Connections   between people
- Associations   between people
- Expectations   between people or individually

The term "contract" is used later in the revelation to refer to this list of words. A contract requires two or more parties. This list of terms represents ways in which people might adopt or claim they are married after this life.

In order for a marriage to be accepted by the Savior, it must be made by "*him who is anointed.*" This marriage must be done in the temple and be performed by one, who has the holy priesthood and are authorization to perform this marriage.

---

[155] D&C 132:7

The Lord said *"All <u>contracts</u>* (referring to the list above) *that are not made unto this end have an end when men are dead."* Unless a marriage is properly administered during mortality, it will not be effective past the death of both individuals. Of necessity, the temple must be available to them. For deceased ancestors we perform this marriage for them in the temple. We do not act as judges in performing or not performing these marriages. The Savior will judge whether the marriage is effective for them. There may be something that is not known, that will make a difference.

Marriage must be performed by "*him who is anointed*." The prophet and President of the Church is the one who has the priesthood keys to perform these marriages. Joseph Smith had those keys at the time this revelation was recorded. We understand now that the President of the Church does not directly perform these sealings although he may and probably does for his family and others of his choosing. Currently temple marriages are performed by those who have been given the authority as authorized by the President of the Church.

Lord's Law

The Savior gave a firm statement about those things created by man. He said the following,

> ***I am the Lord thy God; and I give unto you this commandment**—<u>that no man shall come unto the Father but by me or by my word, which is my law, saith the Lord</u>.*
>
> *And everything that is in the world, whether it be ordained of men, by thrones, or principalities, or powers, or things of name, whatsoever they may be, that are not by me or by my word, saith the Lord,* **shall be thrown down, and shall not remain after men are dead,** *neither in nor after the resurrection, saith the Lord your God.*[156]

If things are not done by the Savior's authority, they will not last into eternity. Eternal Marriage is one of these things that must be done by the Savior's authority to be effective in eternity.

---

[156] D&C 132:12-13

Ministering Servants

If this marriage covenant is rejected, it cannot be restored by later relatives performing the ordinance for them after they are dead. The marriage may be performed, but

> *Therefore, if a man marry him a wife in the world,* **and he marry her not by me nor by my word, and he covenant with her so long as he is in the world and she with him, their covenant and marriage are not of force when they are dead,** <u>and when they are out of the world</u>; *therefore, they are not bound by any law when they are out of the world.*
>
> *Therefore,* **when they are out of the world they neither marry nor are given in marriage; but** <u>**are appointed angels in heaven, which angels are ministering servants,**</u> *to minister for those who are worthy of a far more, and an exceeding, and an eternal weight of glory.*
>
> **For these angels did not abide my law; therefore,** <u>**they cannot be enlarged, but remain separately and singly, without exaltation, in their saved condition**</u>*, to all eternity; and from henceforth are not gods,* <u>**but are angels of God forever and ever.**</u>[157]

When a couple is married, but not by a temple sealing marriage and temples are available to them, their marriage is not valid in eternity, nor is marriage in eternity available to them. If they are otherwise faithful, they are ministering servants or angels for those in the highest degree of the Celestial Kingdom. The temple sealing marriage must be performed in the couple's mortality to be effective.

If their parents were married in the temple by the proper authority and faithful to the end of their lives, they have the promise that they will have their children with them. Then by the parent's marriage covenant, that child will be a ministering angel to them.

However, if one spouse dies, the other spouse may have this temple sealing marriage performed. It is not known whether that couple will be married in eternity. If the deceased person was not a worthy person, it is not likely that this specific marriage is valid. The

---

[157] D&C 132:15-17

deceased spouse would have to have lived a life worthy of that marriage. The living spouse having been faithful and temple married will have the opportunity to have a companion in eternity.

In doing our genealogy we perform all marriages for deceased relatives. We do not judge as there may be circumstances that may make a difference that we do not know. The Savior will be the judge in all of these matters and we need to accept his judgments as they will be just.

This revelation discusses the situation where the couple makes a covenant between themselves that their marriage is for time and all eternity but are not married in the Lord's way. The fact that they made this covenant between themselves and not by the Lord's priesthood does not make a difference for them. Since their marriage is not sealed by priesthood authority, their marriage is not effective beyond their deaths.[158]

This verse also states those not married properly will not be able to pass by the angels and gods who are appointed to guard the entry into the highest degree in the Celestial Kingdom. Only faithful couples, married in the marriage covenant will pass by the angels of heaven. This principle would also apply to those previously described, who were not temple married. This means that they will not inherit eternal life.

This revelation describes the blessings for those who marry properly in the new and everlasting covenant. They shall:

- inherit thrones, kingdoms, principalities, and powers, dominions, all heights and depths
- pass by the angels and the gods which are set there to determine their worthiness to enter.[159]

I had a discussion with one of my wife's roommates. She was perplexed because in her patriarchal blessing she was counseled to not marry out of the temple or the marriage covenant. I had no knowledge at the time of why that was in her patriarchal blessing. She expressed a very strong desire to be married. She did not have any offers of marriage from temple worthy men. She could not

---

[158] D&C 132:18
[159] D&C 132:19

understand why she was counseled to marry in the temple. Several years following our marriage she married a nonmember. She still continued to attend Church and go to the temple. Her husband often attended Church with her but did not join.

Then she developed cancer and died. My understanding is that her husband never joined the Church. If he did not join the Church then this good sister will be a ministering angel to her parents. She had rejected the new and everlasting covenant of marriage. She had not rejected the gospel or the Savior. She was faithful in all but the marriage covenant.

Section 131

This revelation states that there are three heavens or degrees in the Celestial Kingdom. This is important to understand as other things are explained,

> *In the celestial glory there are three heavens or degrees;*
>
> *And in order to obtain the highest, a man must enter into this order of the priesthood [meaning the new and everlasting covenant of marriage];*
>
> **And if he does not, he cannot obtain it.**
>
> **He may enter into the other, but that is the end of his kingdom**; he cannot have an increase. [160]

It is a man's responsibility to be married in the temple. If he does not, he will not obtain the highest degree. A sister is not obligated to accept any marriage proposal, which she deems not suitable for her. If she dies in the faith without marriage, she will be entitled to have that priesthood marriage covenant performed for her during the millennium. When she identifies the companion, she wishes to be with for eternity, then proper arrangements will be made to have that marriage performed.

Section 22 and Marriage Covenant

This revelation contains the exact expression as written in Section 132. It identifies a covenant as "*a new and an everlasting covenant*" and is identical to the expression describing the marriage covenant in

---

[160] D&C 131:1-4

section 132. This phrase refers to the marriage covenant. Normally it is the last covenant in the sequence of covenants we make that will qualify us for eternal life. Verse 3 of that revelation read,

> *For it is because of your dead works that I have caused this last covenant and this church to be built up unto me, even as in days of old.*[161]

The dead works refers to religious works engaged in without the proper priesthood. The Church of Jesus Christ of Latter-Day Saints is the only Church that provides temple marriage. The marriage covenant is normally the last covenant that is performed in the life of a person that qualifies one for eternal life. Once this ordinance is performed both parties must live the principles taught be the Savior for the rest of their lives.

As this Church grows in membership it fulfills the expression *"this church to be built up unto me"*. As more temples are built, then *"this last covenant is built up unto me"*. Because of this, more temple marriages will be performed to qualify members which would qualify them for eternal life. Then more worthy people will be admitted into the presence of the Father and Savior. This is the goal of the Father and the Savior.

This is the proper interpretation of this verse.

Marriage Covenant Children

The First Presidency and Quorum of the Twelve Apostles of the Church issued a proclamation entitled "The Family: A Proclamation to the World." In it is this statement,

> *The divine plan of happiness enables family relationships to be perpetuated beyond the grave. Sacred ordinances and covenants available in holy temples make it possible for individuals to return to the presence of God and for **families to be united eternally**.*

Being united eternally comes from the sealing powers of the marriage covenant. When many talks are given quoting this proclamation, it is interpreted as our single family with no direct reference to grandchildren or great grandchildren.

---

[161] D&C 22:3

The Prophet Joseph Smith recorded the following in his journal dated August 13, 1843, when making comments about Judge Higby's passing:

> *Four destroying angels holding power over the four quarters of the earth until the servants of God are sealed in their foreheads, which signifies sealing the blessing upon their heads, meaning the everlasting covenant, thereby making their calling and election sure.* **When a seal is put upon the father and mother, <u>it secures their posterity</u>, so that they cannot be lost, but will be saved by virtue of the covenant of their father and mother.** [162]

The Family Proclamation references family and is generally interpreted as applying to only our children. Joseph's quote above expressly uses the term "posterity." This is a broader expression than single family members.

Generally, when Joseph spoke, he had a clerk record his message. Upon receiving the written notes, he would review them and put them in his journal sometimes with changes. Willard Richards was his clerk at the time of the above quote. Joseph made an addition to Willard's notes by adding the bolded words above and then published it as a part of his record. The words quoted above are Joseph's direct words.

Joseph's addition is about the sealing powers of the marriage covenant. If parents live faithfully, <u>their posterity</u> will be saved with them by virtue of their marriage covenant. This statement by Joseph Smith does not say what the salvation of their posterity will be but they will not be lost. This is independent of the righteousness of their children because their children *"cannot be lost."* The marriage covenant and faithfulness of the parents will bind their posterity to them.

Posterity

Does it seem right that a wayward child would be with us as we interpret the proclamation and their children (our grandchildren) would be lost because they were not taught properly by our children? Should they be penalized in eternity because of their parents?

---

[162] Smith, History of the Church Vol 5 P 530

The Lord gives us the meaning of "posterity" when he gave a revelation to Joseph Smith. It addressed some principles when many saints were experiencing brutal and terrible atrocities, while being forced from Missouri,

> *And now, verily I say unto you, if that enemy shall escape my vengeance, that he be not brought into judgment before me, then ye shall see to it that ye warn him in my name, that he come no more upon you, **neither upon your family, even your children's children unto the third and fourth generation**.*
>
> *And then, if he shall come upon you or your children, or your children's children unto the third and fourth generation, I have delivered thine enemy into thine hands;*
>
> *And then **if thou wilt spare him**, thou shalt be rewarded for thy righteousness; **and also thy children and thy children's children unto the third and fourth generation**.*[163]

The term posterity in Joseph's statement identified posterity being our descendants unto the *"third and fourth generation."*

However, our posterity does not always accept what we teach and their lives vary in righteousness.

They may,

- accept the gospel principles and marry faithfully in the temple and thereby be worthy of the celestial kingdom based on their own decisions and conduct.
- accept the gospel principles either initially or after repentance and be married but not married in the temple.
- not accept or live the gospel principles and die in their unrepentant state.

There are three degrees of glory or kingdoms to which a person can be consigned by the Savior. They are the Telestial, Terrestrial and the Celestial Kingdoms each having an associated glory. Consignment is based on the level of righteousness of the individual. In the Celestial Kingdom there are also three degrees of glory. Eternal life or life with the Father and the Savior is the highest degree.

---

[163] D&C 98:28-30, see also 98:33-37

The other two degrees are identified in the following verse,

> *In the celestial glory there are three heavens or degrees*[164]

The term "heaven" suggests that these degrees are places of residence for the eternities. We do not have revelations clearly identifying who will inherit the Second and third heavens.

If we as parents are faithful and inherit eternal life, then we are entitled to have our posterity up to the third or fourth generation with us. This group will be identified as our family. If our family member has entered the marriage covenant and kept the commandments faithfully to the end of their lives, they will inherit the highest degree in the Celestial Kingdom. They will be with us.

If our posterity member is faithful, trying to keep the covenants and marries but not in the marriage covenant, they will be a ministering angel. It is expected they will be in the second kingdom or glory. They have a level of faithfulness but do not qualify to be with us as equals in the Celestial Kingdom.

Our wayward posterity is expected to be consigned to the third kingdom or degree. Their lives were not righteous enough to be with those in the second kingdom.

Our Wayward Posterity

Elder Orson F. Whitney taught what Joseph Smith taught as,

> *The Prophet Joseph Smith declared and he never taught more comforting doctrine that the eternal sealings of faithful parents and the divine promises made to them for valiant service in the Cause of Truth, would save not only themselves, **but likewise their posterity**. **Though some of the sheep may wander, the eye of the Shepherd is upon them, and sooner or later they will feel the tentacles of Divine Providence reaching out after them and drawing them back to the fold.** Either in this life or the life to come, they will return. **They will have to pay their debt to justice; they will suffer for their sins.*** [165]

---

[164] D&C 131:1

[165] Whitney, Church Conference Report, April 1929, P 110

This statement confirms that posterity and not just our immediate children are saved. There are two other primary principles in this statement.

- The Savior will reach out to those who are wayward to draw them back into righteousness.
- If they die in their sins, they will have to pay their debt to justice. They will suffer for their sins.

It is comforting to faithful parents to know that the Father and the Savior will provide events which will encourage wayward posterity to return to righteousness. We must remember that our posterity has their agency and may choose not to respond to those promptings.

If the wayward posterity responds to the "*tentacles of Divine Providence*" and sincerely repent they will be forgiven. Depending on their marital status they will be in the highest degree of the Celestial Kingdom or a ministering angel.

The wayward posterity that doesn't respond to the "*tentacles of Divine Providence*" and die in their sins will have to "*pay their debt to justice.*" They will pay for their sins in the same way that every other mortal pays for their sins. They will have to suffer in hell following their death.

Amulek taught the Zoramites,

> *For behold, if ye have procrastinated the day of your repentance even until death,* **behold, ye have become subjected to the spirit of the devil, and he doth seal you his ; therefore, the Spirit of the Lord hath withdrawn from you, and hath no place in you, and the devil hath all power over you** [166]

Unrepentant posterity will become subject unto Satan when they die. They suffer in hell and will suffer the buffetings and torment of Satan in hell and the everlasting fire. All of them will be resurrected in their time. When they are resurrected, they will have paid for their sins and receive forgiveness. They will no longer suffer the buffetings of Satan after their resurrection. This is confirmed in the following verse that speaks of the suffering from Satan,

---

[166] Alma 34:35

> *Nevertheless, it is not written that there shall be no end to this torment,* [167]

These wayward posterity family members will be consigned to the lowest kingdom or degree of glory in the Celestial Kingdom. However, they will be with their faithful parents as that kingdom is a part of the Celestial kingdom.

PROBATIONARY LIFE

Our mortal life is a probationary period during which we can repent. Alma in explaining this probationary period to Zeezrom and the people of Ammonihah said,

> *And we see that death comes upon mankind, yea, the death which has been spoken of by Amulek, which is the temporal death; nevertheless **there was a space granted unto man in which he might repent**; therefore **this life became a probationary state; a time to prepare to meet God**; a time to prepare for that endless state which has been spoken of by us, <u>which is after the resurrection of the dead</u>.*[168]

Nephi explained the same concept,

> *The day should come that they must be judged of their works, yea, even **the works which were done by the temporal body in their days of probation**.*[169]

This probationary period ends at our death. Then we will be judged on our activities, attitudes, and righteousness during this mortal period according to the gospel knowledge available to us.

What is being taught in the scriptures is that we will be judged on the works and attitudes we performed during our mortal probation. This applies to all people, when the knowledge of the Savior is available in their society. If the knowledge of the Savior is available, we will be held accountable for not living the Savior's principles. For those who do not have access to the gospel, they have the opportunity to repent in the world of spirits.

---

[167] D&C 19:4-6
[168] Alma 12:24, 2 Nephi 2:21, 2 Nephi 9:27, 2 Nephi 33:9, Helaman 13:38,
[169] 1 Nephi 15:32

ETERNAL LIFE

The expression "eternal life" and "everlasting life" have the same meaning. They are found numerous times in the scriptures. There are occasions where language is used which refers to eternal life but does not use these exact terms. A recent count of the scriptures where these two terms are use is,

	EL	EVL	Total
• New Testament	19	51	70
• Book of Mormon	16	56	72
• Doctrine and Covenants	7	59	66
• Old Testament	2	0	2
• Pearl of Great Price	0	10	10

What does it mean to qualify for eternal life? The Savior said the following about the end of the earth. This describes a final resurrection and is the last resurrection that will occur. It will happen just prior to the earth passing away. It will include all of those still in hell with Satan. This is determined by the expression *"yea, even all."*

> *But, behold, verily I say unto you, before the earth shall pass away, Michael, mine archangel, shall sound his trump, and then shall all the dead awake, for their graves shall be opened, and they shall come forth—yea, even all.*
>
> *And the righteous shall be gathered on **my right hand unto eternal life**; and the **wicked on my left hand** will I be ashamed to own before the Father;*[170]

The first paragraph describes the last resurrection including those in hell at the end of the millennium. When this resurrection occurs all of the Father's children will have been resurrected. Then he states that the righteous will have eternal life with him. All others are referred to as wicked. They are wicked as to being worthy to be in the presence of the Father and the Savior.

However, parents worthy of eternal life will have claim on their posterity to be with them in the Celestial Kingdom. Unless their posterity is worthy of eternal life, they will not be in the presence of the Father and the Savior, but they will be in the presence of their

---

[170] D&C 29:26-27

parents. They will be in one of the two lower degrees or habitation in the Celestial Kingdom.

Progression

Many of us view and wonder how we could be like the Savior or the Father when we die. We look at the Savior's life and compare ourselves with him and see a big difference. Will we be worthy enough to be in their presence? Joseph Smith made some remarks that help us to better understand how we progress.

> *Here, then, is eternal life—to know the only wise and true God; and you have got to learn how to be gods yourselves, and to be kings and priests to God, the same as all gods have done before you, namely, by going from one small degree to another, and from a small capacity to a great one; from grace to grace, from exaltation to exaltation, until you attain to the resurrection of the dead, and are able to dwell in everlasting burnings, and to sit in glory, as do those who sit enthroned in everlasting power.*[171]

And following this he said,

> *When you climb up a ladder, you must begin at the bottom, and ascend step by step, until you arrive at the top; and so it is with the principles of the gospel—you must begin with the first, and **go on until you learn all the principles of exaltation**. <u>But it will be a great while after you have passed through the veil before you will have learned them.</u> It is not all to be comprehended in this world; **it will be a great work to learn our salvation and exaltation even beyond the grave**.*[172]

But all of us have to take the first step in this progression in this life. If we are eligible for eternal life, we will continue our quest to become like our Father and the Savior. Each of us will progress until we have learned all we need to know about exaltation. Then we will attain the status of God. But we must start on this journey in this life, if it is available to us. We do this by being a member of his Church and trying to become like him.

WORLD of SPIRITS

---

[171] History of the Church, Vol 6, P 305 - BYU Studies
[172] History of the Church, Vol 6, P 306 – BYU Studies

When we die our spirit body separate from our physical body. Joseph Smith had this to say about where our spirit goes,

> *I will say something about the spirits in prison. There has been much said by modern divines about the words of Jesus to the thief, saying, 'This day shalt thou be with me in paradise.' King James' translators make it out to say paradise. But what is paradise? It is a modern word it does not answer at all to the original word that Jesus made use of.* **There is nothing in the original word in Greek froze [from] which this was taken that signifies paradise; but it was-<u>This day thou shalt be with me in the world of spirits</u>** *"* [173]

Then at a different time he said,

> *There has been much said about the word hell, and the sectarian world have preached much about it, describing it to be a burning lake of fire and brimstone. But what is hell? It is another modern term, and is taken from hades.*
>
> **Hades, the Greek, or Shaole, the Hebrew: these two significations mean a world of spirits. Hades, Shaole, paradise, spirits in prison, are all one: it is a world of spirits.**
>
> <u>**The righteous and the wicked all go to the same world of spirits until the resurrection.**</u> [174]

This world of spirits has both righteous and wicked people in it. At a conference in Nauvoo Joseph Smith made some comments about James Adams during which he said,

> *He had had revelations concerning his departure, and had gone to a more important work – of opening up a more effectual door for the dead.* **The spirits of the just are exalted to a greater and more glorious work** *–hence they are blessed in departing hence.* <u>**Enveloped in flaming fire,**</u> **they are not far from us, and know and understand our thoughts, feelings and [e]motions, and are often pained therewith.***"* [175]

---

[173] Smith, History of the Church, Vol 5, P 425
[174] Smith, History of the Church, Vol 5 25
[175] Ehat, Words of Joseph Smith, 253-254

The just people are enveloped in flaming fire? This may be new to some, but Lehi and Nephi nevertheless saw this flaming fire attribute of the just in their vision of the tree of life. After his marvelous vision Lehi told part of his vision to his family and expressed serious concern for Laman and Lemuel because they had not partaken of the precious fruit. Afterwards the brothers were discussing Lehi's comments and Nephi explained many things to his brothers. During his comments to his brothers, he said this,

> *And I said unto them that it was an awful gulf, which separated the wicked from the tree of life, and also from the saints of God.*
>
> *And I said unto them that it was a representation of that awful hell, which the angel said unto me was prepared for the wicked.*
>
> *And I said unto them that our father also saw that the justice of God did also divide the wicked from the righteous; and the **brightness thereof was like unto the brightness of a flaming fire, which ascendeth up unto God forever and ever, and hath no end.*** [176]

This quote about flaming fire refers to the spirits of the just who have a brightness that radiates from them. When a person dies, he is received either into paradise with a glory of brightness like a flaming fire, which is a state of happiness, peace and rest, or into spirit prison. The unrepentant are in a state which we refer to as hell. This hell is suffering under Satan's control and is in the world of spirits.

The Wicked

The term "wicked" has been used in the scriptures that identify two different gospel concepts and consequently refers to two different groups of people.

Group 1

The Lord describes those who will inherit the Telestial Kingdom,

> *These are they who are liars, and sorcerers, and adulterers, and whoremongers, and whosoever loves and makes a lie.*
>
> *These are they who suffer the **wrath of God** on earth.*

---

[176] 1 Nephi 15:28-30

*These are they who suffer the **vengeance of eternal fire.**[177]*

Notice the kinds of sins committed by the wicked which are adultery, fornication, liars, etc. These are sins that send a soul to hell in the World of Spirits and eventually to the Telestial Kingdom, unless claimed by righteous parents.

The above list of sins does not identify all of the sins that will qualify us for hell. Abinadi has identified a more complete list of sins, which he read to King Noah and his followers,

> *And now I read unto you the remainder of the commandments of God, for I perceive that they are not written in your hearts; I perceive that ye have studied and taught iniquity the most part of your lives.*

> *And now, ye remember that I said unto you: Thou shalt not make unto thee any graven image, or any likeness of things which are in heaven above, or which are in the earth beneath, or which are in the water under the earth.*

> *And again: Thou shalt not bow down thyself unto them, nor serve them; for I the Lord thy God am a jealous God, visiting the iniquities of the fathers upon the children, unto the third and fourth generations of them that hate me;*

> *And showing mercy unto thousands of them that love me and keep my commandments.*

> *Thou shalt not take the name of the Lord thy God in vain; for the Lord will not hold him guiltless that taketh his name in vain.*

> *Remember the sabbath day, to keep it holy.*

> *Six days shalt thou labor, and do all thy work;*

> *But the seventh day, the sabbath of the Lord thy God, thou shalt not do any work, thou, nor thy son, nor thy daughter, thy man-servant, nor thy maid-servant, nor thy cattle, nor thy stranger that is within thy gates;*

> *For in six days the Lord made heaven and earth, and the sea, and all that in them is; wherefore the Lord blessed the sabbath day, and hallowed it.*

---

[177] D&C 75:103-105

> *Honor thy father and thy mother, that thy days may be long upon the land which the Lord thy God giveth thee.*
>
> *Thou shalt not kill.*
>
> *Thou shalt not commit adultery. Thou shalt not steal.*
>
> *Thou shalt not bear false witness against thy neighbor.*
>
> *Thou shalt not covet thy neighbor's house, thou shalt not covet thy neighbor's wife, nor his man-servant, nor his maid-servant, nor his ox, nor his ass, nor anything that is thy neighbor's.*[178]

Of course, we can repent of these sins in mortality except for the taking of life. But, where these principles are taught in a society of prophets and are generally known, then those that do not live these teachings are held accountable by the Savior,

> *And, again, I say unto you, that whoso having knowledge, have I not commanded to repent?*[179]

Whether a person acknowledges his sins or not he is still held accountable if he does not repent,

> *And it shall come to pass, because of the wickedness of the world, that I will take vengeance upon the wicked, **for they will not repent**; for the cup of mine indignation is full; **for behold, my blood shall not cleanse them if they hear me not**.*[180]

As members of the Church, we need to have continual faith in the Savior. If we fail, then,

> *And he that endureth not unto the end, the same is he that is also hewn down and cast into the fire [suffering everlasting fire], from whence **they can no more return**, because of the justice of the Father.*[181]

Recognize that these cannot return to the state that they had. In other words, they cannot repent in the world of spirits and be eligible for eternal life. They still have the opportunity to repent up until their death. They had the opportunity in mortality and started on the

---

[178] Mosiah 13:11-24
[179] D&C 29:49
[180] D&C 29:17, See Mosiah 3:20-22
[181] 3 Nephi 27:17

journey but did not continue that path. These will be cast into or experience everlasting fire [Read Everlasting Fire page 94].

Abinadi taught King Noah and his priests,

> *But behold, and fear, and tremble before God, for ye ought to tremble*; **for the Lord redeemeth none such that rebel against him and die in their sins; yea, even all those that have perished in their sins ever since the world began, <u>that have wilfully rebelled against God, that have known the commandments of God, and would not keep them; these are they that have no part in the first resurrection.</u>** [182]

Abinadi taught in this quote that if a person, regardless of when they lived, dies in their sins, they have *"<u>wilfully rebelled against God</u>"* they will not have *"part in the first resurrection"* The expression *"<u>wilfully rebelled against God</u>"* means that his gospel was available to them and they rejected living it.

Those who have no part in the first resurrection are those who are committed to hell suffering the buffetings of Satan until the final resurrection. There is no repentance available to them for they had their opportunity to fully repent in mortality. These are wicked people and will be resurrected at the time of the final judgment because they are not worthy to be resurrected as part of the *"first resurrection."*

Group 2

This group is identified from the following scripture given by the Savior,

> *But, behold, verily I say unto you, before the earth shall pass away, Michael, mine archangel, shall sound his trump, and* ***then shall all the dead awake, for their graves shall be opened, and they shall come forth—yea, even all.***
>
> *And the righteous shall be gathered on <u>my right hand unto eternal life</u>; and the* ***wicked on my left hand*** *will I be ashamed to own before the Father;*
>
> *Wherefore I will say unto them—**Depart from me, ye cursed, into everlasting fire, prepared for the devil and his angels**.* [183]

---

[182] Mosiah 15:26
[183] D&C 29:26-28

The first paragraph identifies the event that will happen at the end of the millennium. It describes the last resurrection, which are those who are in hell. Following this is the time that all mankind will be consigned eternally to a kingdom, outer darkness or claimed by parents who were worthy of eternal life.

In this quote, the Savior identifies two groups of people. One group are those worthy of eternal life. All others he identifies as wicked. Think of this for a moment. If you do not have eternal life, you are wicked. This wicked term identified all who cannot enter the Celestial Kingdom and be in the presence of the Father and the Savior. They are wicked because they cannot be in the presence of the Father and Savior. This is **not** because they have committed wicked sins such as lying, stealing, or adultery. It is because they have rejected the marriage covenant. Therefore, they have not received eternal life.

The Savior then states that they will suffer everlasting fire. [Read Everlasting Fire page 94] They are wicked because they are NOT worthy to be in the presence of the Father and Savior. They may however be with their parents who are worthy of eternal life in the Celestial Kingdom.

The Rebellious

President Joseph F. Smith had vision in which he saw the Savior visit the righteous, who had accepted his teachings and were in the world of spirits.[184] These righteous people were all of those who lived and died prior to the Savior's death.

In addition, there would be a very large group of people who had not heard of the Savior and needed to be taught the gospel. The Savior did not appear to these people. The Savior organized the righteous to teach these people.

President Smith wrote,

> *But unto the **wicked** he did not go, and among the **ungodly and the unrepentant who had defiled themselves while in the flesh, his voice was not raised;***

---

[184] D&C 138

*Neither did the **rebellious** who rejected the testimonies and the warnings of the ancient prophets behold his presence, nor look upon his face.*

Where these were, darkness reigned, but among the righteous there was peace; [185]

This scripture identifies two groups, the wicked and the rebellious. Both groups were where darkness reigns. This would be in hell subject to Satan. The first group is the wicked who had the gospel teachings available to them but "*defiled themselves*" with their sins. This group was addressed above in Group 1 in the above section and have no opportunity to repent in the world of spirits.[186]

The second group is identified as the rebellious. They rejected the message of the "*ancient prophets.*" Both groups were in darkness meaning they were in hell subject to Satan. That is because both groups had rejected the testimonies and warnings of prophets and were subject to Satan and his hosts in the world of spirits.

Who was this rebellious group that rejected "*ancient prophets*"?

President Smith was reading in 1 Peter which started this spiritual query that led to this revelation. Peter wrote;

*By which also he went and **preached unto the spirits in prison;***

*Which sometime were **disobedient, when once the longsuffering of God waited in the days of Noah,** while the ark was a preparing, wherein few, that is, eight souls were saved by water.*[187]

Peter identifies a people who were disobedient at the time of Noah and were in spirit prison. They were in spirit prison because they did not listen to prophets during their mortal life. A review of the events in the days of Noah will identify these rebellious people.

The Lord was preparing the earth for its baptism of water in which the earth would be covered with water. The Lord had commanded Noah to build an Arc for the safety of his family and the animals he put on the arc with him.

---

[185] D&C 138:20-22.
[186] D&C 76:84-85
[187] 1 Peter 3:19-20

Also, at this time, Enoch[188] had been called directly as a prophet and was preaching to the inhabitants during the time Noah was building his arc. Many repented and followed Enoch and those that repented became known as "Zion", a righteous people. Because the floods that were coming, God took Enoch and Zion from the earth to heaven. After Enoch was gone from the earth, an unrepentant group of people were left and were drowned in the floods. This group that drowned are identified as the rebellious. They lived at the time of Noah and were placed in hell because they did not repent and join Zion. These were the ones that Peter identified as being preached to in the world of spirits. These were the people that Joseph F. Smith identified as the rebellious.

Joseph Smith and Sidney Rigdon saw in vision those who inherit or will be placed to the Telestial, Terrestrial and Celestial Kingdoms[189]. In their revelation on those who will inherit the Terrestrial Kingdom, it is recorded:

> *And also they who are the **spirits of men kept in prison**, whom the Son visited, and preached the gospel unto them, that they might be judged according to men in the flesh;*
>
> ***Who received not the testimony of Jesus in the flesh, but afterwards received it**[190]*

This describes persons who are in prison or subject to Satan in the world of spirits and they have the gospel preached to them. What will they receive for their repentance in the world of spirits? They will receive the *"testimony of Jesus"*, which they did not receive in their mortality. In other words, they will believe in and accept the salvation that Jesus Christ provided in his atonement. They do not receive the "fulness of the Father", which are the blessings of the temple because they rejected that opportunity in their mortal lives. Their reward from this acceptance is that they will be consigned to the Terrestrial Kingdom. If the rebellious do not repent or accept the testimony of the Savior, when it is preached to them in the world of spirits, their eternal place is the Telestial Kingdom unless claimed by worthy parents.

---

[188] Moses Chap 7-8

[189] D&C Section 76

[190] D&C 76:73-74

The rebellious cannot be placed in the Celestial Kingdom since they rejected the prophets while in mortality. But by receiving the *"testimony of Jesus"* in the world of spirits they can become inhabitants of the Terrestrial Kingdom which improves their eternal station.

Following Enoch and Zion being taken, there were no righteous people left except Noah and his family. There were no friends or associates living the gospel to set an example and encourage those that remained to be righteous. Perhaps because they did not have that opportunity, God has given them an opportunity to repent in the world of spirits to improve their eternal salvation. These rebellious souls, living at the time of Noah, is the only group in the history of the world that are in spirit prison, that have the opportunity to repent and improve their eternal salvation.

The Savior organized the faithful spirits to preach the gospel in the world of spirits. President Smith recorded,

> *But behold, from among the righteous, he organized his forces and appointed messengers, clothed with power and authority, and commissioned them to go forth and carry the, even to all the light of the gospel to them that were in darkness spirits of men; and thus was the gospel preached to the dead.* [191]

The message that some will get from this language is that "all" of the "spirits of men" who are in darkness, or in hell" will have the gospel preached to them. This is not compatible with many other scriptures. Actually, there is one group of people in hell that will have the gospel preached to them but certainly not all. This group of people are identified as "Rebellious".

The Book of Mormon is very clear, the wicked who have the gospel available to them will not have the opportunity to repent in the world of spirits. They are committed to the power of Satan until their resurrection. The contents of the following quote are typical,

> *we must come forth and stand before him in his glory, and in his power, and in his might, majesty, and dominion, and acknowledge to our everlasting shame that all his judgments are just; that he is just in all his works, and that he is merciful unto*

---

[191] D&C 138:30

the children of men, and that he has all power to save every man that believeth on his name and bringeth forth fruit meet for repentance.

And now behold, I say unto you then cometh a death, even a second death, which is a spiritual death; then is a time that whosoever dieth in his sins, as to a temporal death, shall also die a spiritual death; yea, he shall die as to things pertaining unto righteousness.

Then is the time when their torments shall be as a lake of fire and brimstone, whose flame ascendeth up forever and ever; and then is the time that they shall be chained down to an everlasting destruction, according to the power and captivity of Satan, he having subjected them according to his will.[192]

Everlasting Fire

This everlasting Fire will be experienced by all who are not entitled to eternal life but had the opportunity to qualify for it,

And the righteous shall be gathered on **my right hand unto eternal life**; *and the* **wicked on my left hand** *will I be ashamed to own before the Father;*

*Wherefore I will say unto them—****Depart from me, ye cursed, into everlasting fire, prepared for the devil and his angels.***[193]

King Benjamin was visited by an angel[194] who described the coming of the Savior to the earth. The angel spoke of the Savior's earthly visit and the miracles and blessings he would give to the people. He described the Savior's bleeding in the garden, scourging and crucifixion. The angel further described some of the judgments that would be happening if the people did not repent and be worthy to return to the Father's presence. This message was taught to his people as he was commanded to do.[195]

King Benjamin described the judgment that the unrepentant would suffer,

---

[192] Alma 12:15-17
[193] D&C 29:27-28
[194] Mosiah 3:2
[195] Mosiah 3:3-23

> *And **if they be evil they are consigned to an awful view of their own guilt and abominations**, <u>which doth cause them to shrink from the presence of the Lord into a state of misery and endless torment,</u> **from whence they can no more return;** <u>therefore they have drunk damnation to their own souls.</u>*
>
> *And **their torment is as a lake of fire and brimstone, whose flames are unquenchable, and whose smoke ascendeth up forever and ever.**[196]*

This angel identified people who are classified as *evil*. This quote describes something that each individual will suffer. Each such individual is *"consigned to an awful view of **their own guilt and abominations.**"* They will *"shrink from the presence of the Lord in a state of misery and endless torment."*

They cannot change their situation. To state it differently they cannot repent from their situation. They had their opportunity in mortality because they had knowledge of the Savior[197] and did not conduct themselves so that they could avoid this fire.

The Prophet Joseph Smith understood this torment and said,

> *The great misery of departed spirits in the world of spirits, where they go after death, **is to know that they come short of the glory that others enjoy and that they might have enjoyed themselves**, and **they are their own accusers**[198]*

And also

> *A man is his own tormentor and his own condemner. Hence the saying, They shall go into the lake that burns with fire and brimstone. **<u>The torment of disappointment in the mind of man is as exquisite as a lake burning with fire and brimstone.</u>**[199]*

Joseph identifies that departed spirits will know in the world of spirits, prior to their resurrection, that they have fallen short of the glory they might have received. Their *"disappointment"* will be a torment that will be as a *"lake burning with fire and brimstone*

---

[196] Mosiah 3:25, 27, See also Mosiah 5:5

[197] Mosiah 3:20-22

[198] Smith, History of the Church 5:425

[199] Smith, History of the Church 6:314

Our children not worthy of eternal life will suffer this torment of everlasting fire. If we have taught them properly, and their lives are such that they are not worthy of eternal life then they must suffer this torment. At their resurrection they will be forgiven and that torment will pass. The Savior said of this torment,

> *Nevertheless, it is not written that there shall be no end to* ***this torment***, [200]

The Lord describes those who inherit the Telestial Kingdom,

> *These are they who suffer the* ***vengeance of eternal fire.***

Their torment will be extreme as they suffer it. It should be mentioned that sons of perdition will experience this torment throughout eternity because they have no forgiveness.

Our children not qualified for eternal life will suffer this torment until their resurrection when they receive forgiveness and are claimed by worthy parents.

No Knowledge of Truth

President Smith recorded an interesting statement in his revelation.

> *Thus was* ***the gospel preached to those who had died in their sins, without a knowledge of the truth,*** [201]

It identifies a group of people who have no "*knowledge of the truth."* They knew nothing of the Savior and his atonement during their mortality. Yet they "died in their sins".

Paul *said,*

> *sin is not imputed when there is no law.*[202]

What is really being said here is that where there is no law or gospel, people are not held accountable for their conduct. This is further explained by Jacob. Nephi wrote of Jacob's teachings,

> ***where there is no law given there is no punishment; and where there is no punishment there is no condemnation; and where there is no condemnation the mercies of the Holy One of Israel***

---

[200] D&C 19:4-6
[201] D&C 138:32
[202] Romans 5:13, 4:15

*have claim upon them, **because of the atonement**; for they are delivered by the power of him.*

*For the **atonement satisfieth the demands of his justice** upon all those who have not the law given to them, that **they are delivered from** that awful monster, **death and hell, and the devil, and <u>the lake of fire and brimstone, which is endless torment</u>**; and **they are restored to that God who gave them breath, which is the Holy One of Israel**.*[203]

The Savior's atonement provides those who have no law with two judgments which are,

- *they are delivered from that awful monster, death and hell, and the devil, and the lake of fire and brimstone, which is endless torment.*
- *they are restored to that God who gave them breath, which is the Holy One of Israel.*

They will be consigned to the Terrestrial Kingdom and are,

they who died without law[204]

The Savior will minister to those in the Terrestrial Kingdom,

*These are they **who receive of the presence of the Son**, but not of the fulness of the Father.*

Wherefore, they are bodies terrestrial.[205]

However, these people can repent and receive the full blessing of the temple. President Smith records,

These were taught faith in God, repentance from sin, vicarious baptism for the remission of sins, the gift of the Holy Ghost by the laying on of hands,

And all other principles of the gospel that were necessary for them to know in order to qualify themselves that they might be judged

---

[203] 2 Nephi 9:25–26; Moroni 8:22
[204] D&C 76:72
[205] D&C 76:77-78

according to men in the flesh, but live according to God in the spirit.[206]

However, if they do not accept this message they will be consigned to the Terrestrial world.

Honorable Men/Women

This section will begin by comparing the conduct of these people with those suffering in hell. Those who suffer in hell are,

> *These are they who are liars, and sorcerers, and adulterers, and whoremongers, and whosoever loves and makes a lie.*
>
> *These are they who suffer the wrath of God on earth.*
>
> *These are they who suffer the vengeance of eternal fire.*
>
> *These are they who are cast down to hell and suffer the wrath of Almighty God, until the fulness of times*[207]

Honorable men are identified as those who will inherit the Terrestrial Kingdom. The wording of the revelation that identifies these men and women is,

> *honorable men of the earth, who were blinded by the craftiness of men.*[208]

The term honorable is used by the Savior in describing those whom he classifies as honorable. The definition of honorable then must be interpreted in light of the Savior's standards. The definition of honorable is,

> *in accordance with or characterized by principles of honor*[209]

So, honorable men and women would be those who live principles that the Savior would consider honorable. They would be generally honest, faithful to their word, law abiding and concerned and helpful to other people. Their views of religion were probably shaped or *"blinded by the craftiness of men."*

---

[206] D&C 138:33-34
[207] D&C 76:103-106
[208] D&C 76:75
[209] Honorable: Free Online Dictionary

They did not sin such as to qualify them to be in hell. If the gospel was available to them during their life, they will inherit the terrestrial kingdom. If the gospel was not available to them, they will have the gospel preached to them in the world of spirits. but will be in the Terrestrial Kingdom if they do not accept it.

Buffetings of Satan

The expression "buffetings of Satan" is found five (5) times in the Doctrine and Covenants. It does not appear in any other scriptures.

The term "buffetings" appears in modern dictionaries and is defined as a "shaking of an airplane." Those who have flown in turbulent weather know that some airplanes can be tossed about, sometimes violently. The passengers, if not using seat belts, can be thrown out of their seats.

The root word "buffet" has several meanings. From several dictionaries the applicable common meaning is:

1. A blow, especially by the fist
2. Something that affects like a blow

This root word is used in the New Testament to describe abuse to the Savior,

*Then did they spit in his face, **and buffeted him**; and **others smote him with the palms of their hands**,*

Saying, Prophesy unto us, thou Christ, Who is he that smote thee?[210]

These quotes make a difference between the tormentors slapping the Savior with the palm of their hands and hitting him with their fists. When they "buffeted him", they used their fists as the definition indicates. However, from the above quote where they smote him with the palms of their hands, this slap was strongly administered.

The term "buffetings of Satan" is some sort of turbulence, agitation or happening that comes directly from Satan. It would be something powerful like a physical blow or a strong happening. This is something that Satan will inflict. The Savior referred to this "buffeting" but used different terms. He told Peter,

---

[210] Matthew 26:67-68

> *And the Lord said, Simon, Simon, behold,* **Satan hath desired to have you, that he may sift you as wheat:**
>
> *But I have prayed for thee,* **that thy faith fail not***: and when thou art converted, strengthen thy brethren.*[211]

This scripture references Peter's activities after the Savior's resurrection and not those prior to the Savior's death.

In the Savior's time the harvest of wheat was completed by putting the wheat and chaff into baskets and tossing the mixture into the air to separate the wheat chaff from the kernels. This method has been used for a long time. Although this action separates the chaff and the kernels, this tossing activity puts the wheat kernels into constant motion or turbulence. This properly characterizes the "buffetings of Satan." When people suffer the buffetings of Satan in mortality their lives are in a constant turmoil.

The Savior prayed that Peter's "faith, fail not." If Peter did not continue in faith he would not endure to the end. If Peter would have turned from the faith, he would then suffer the *"buffetings of Satan"* or be *"sifted as wheat."* If a person exercises true faith, they get rid of the chaff or sins through repentance.

The Savior gave the Nephites the same warning,

> *he turned again unto the multitude and said unto them:*
>
> *Behold, verily, verily, I say unto you, ye must watch and pray always lest ye enter into temptation; for* **Satan desireth to have you, that he may sift you as wheat**.[212]

These buffetings of Satan can begin in our mortal lives but have a consequence following this life. The Prophet Joseph Smith wrote of a Brother Draper who is believed to be William Draper,

> *In the afternoon we had an exhortation and communion service. Some two or three weeks since, Brother Draper insisted on leaving the meeting before communion, and could not be prevailed on to tarry a few moments, although we invited him to do so, as we did not wish to have the house thrown into confusion. He observed that he "would not," if we excluded him*

---

[211] Luke 22:31-32
[212] 3 Nephi 18:17-18

> *from the Church. Today he attempted to make a confession, but it was not satisfactory to me, and* **I was constrained by the Spirit to deliver him over to the buffetings of Satan, until he should humble himself and repent of his sins, and make satisfactory confession before the Church.**[213]

Joseph's purpose was to spur him to repentance so that he could rejoin in full activity. Paul did this same thing as he recorded in his letter to Timothy,

> *This charge I commit unto thee, son Timothy, according to the prophecies which went before on thee, that thou by them mightest war a good warfare;*
>
> *Holding faith, and a good conscience; which some having put away concerning faith have made shipwreck:*
>
> **Of whom is Hymenæus and Alexander; whom I have delivered unto Satan, that they may learn not to blaspheme.**[214]

William W. Phelps and John Whitmer were sustained as Presidents of the Church in Missouri and were later dismissed by a united vote of the Church. William W. Phelps and John Whitmer were claiming some $2000 of Church funds as their own funds. A court was held,

> *it was decided that William W. Phelps and John Whitmer be no longer members of the Church of Christ of Latter-day Saints, and* **be given over to the buffetings of Satan, until they learn to blaspheme no more against the authorities of God, nor fleece the flock of Christ***.*
>
> *The vote was then put to the congregation, and was carried unanimously.*[215]

William W. Phelps did repent, asking forgiveness of the Church members and those that he offended. He was forgiven. After he rejoined the Church in 1840, he penned fifteen (15) poetic pieces which were set to music and currently appear in the Church Hymnbook. Perhaps the most notable is the hymn "Praise to the

---

[213] Smith, History of the Church, 2:326
[214] 1 Timothy 1:18-20
[215] Smith, History of the Church, 3:8 (See pages 6-8)

Man" giving honor and recognition to the Prophet Joseph Smith whom he had offended and of whom he had spoken evil.

John Whitmer did not repent of his transgressions and retained records of the history of the Church that he had while serving as clerk.[216] He assisted those who were commissioned by the authorities of Missouri to see that the Saints were removed from Missouri.

On 5 April 1839, he and seven (7) others including the county judge met with Theodore Turley who had been working through the legal process to get those in Liberty jail released. This committee was part of the group that was commissioned to see that the Saints were removed from the State of Missouri. John Whitmer had provided this committee a copy of the revelation[217] that stated that the apostles should dedicate the Far West temple site on 26 April 1839. This event was to take place just three weeks from the time of this committee meeting with Theodore Turley.

Brother Turley was told that if the apostles came, they would be murdered to which he jumped up and said "*In the name of God that revelation will be fulfilled.*" He was derided for his statement and they charged him to deny his position and join them. Brother Turley then asked John Whitmer what his position was. In response, John Whitmer did say he saw and handled the plates and described them but said he did not know whether the translation was correct. He was aiding this mob committee, providing them information on which they could act and perhaps murder the apostles. He contradicted his previous testimony that he had given when active in the Church.[218] According to the Church Court's ruling above John Whitmer was turned over to suffer the buffetings of Satan and he did not repent.

The missionary group of apostles met just after midnight on 5 April 1839 and dedicated the Far West temple site thus fulfilling the revelation. They completed their business and then left for their missions as they had previously determined.

As mentioned earlier, there are five (5) occurrences of the expression "buffetings of Satan" in the Doctrine and Covenants. All of these references concern members of the Church who have broken

---

[216] Smith, History of the Church, 6:66

[217] D&C Sect. 118

[218] Smith, History of the Church, 3:307

covenants, transgressed or sinned. Three of those references have a common expression. The offender,

> ...*shall be delivered over to the* **buffetings of Satan until the day of redemption.**[219]

One other quote identifies that the transgressor

> ...*cannot escape the* **buffetings of Satan until the day of redemption.**[220]

These quotes show that there is an end to the buffetings of Satan even if there is no repentance. If the person repents, the buffetings will end. The day of redemption for William W. Phelps was the day he repented and returned to the Church.

If there is no repentance, the day of redemption occurs when that individual is resurrected. When a person suffers the buffetings of Satan and dies, he becomes subject to Satan until his resurrection. His redemption will occur when he is resurrected, forgiven and released from the influence of Satan.

Savior's Teaching and Organization

In the world of spirits, the Savior preached to the gathered faithful. The fundamental doctrines included,

> *the everlasting gospel, the doctrine of the resurrection and the redemption of humankind from the fall, and from individual sins on conditions of repentance.*[221]

In addition to the teachings the Savior presented, he gave these faithful spirits the power to be resurrected after he left the world of spirits,

> *These the Lord taught, and* **gave them power to come forth**, *after his resurrection from the dead, to enter into his Father's kingdom, there to be crowned with immortality and eternal life."*[222]

---

[219] D&C 78:12; 82:21; 132:26
[220] D&C 104:9
[221] D&C 138:18-19
[222] D&C 138:51

The "power to come forth" was the power to be resurrected. After the Savior left the group and completed his own resurrection, many others exercised this power of resurrection. Matthew wrote,

> *The graves were opened; and many bodies of the saints which slept arose,*
>
> *And came out of the graves after his resurrection, and went into the holy city, and appeared unto many.* [223]

President Smith records that the Savior "organized his forces." This means that someone was placed in authority to preside over the work of teaching in the world of spirits. Then there were those who did the actual proselyting. Even now new faithful spirits arrive in the world of spirits to add to the number of commissioned elders to preach the gospel,

> *I beheld that the faithful elders of this dispensation, when they depart from mortal life, continue their labors in the preaching of the gospel of repentance and redemption, through the sacrifice of the Only Begotten Son of God,*[224]

Just Men Made Perfect

There is another group of righteous men that do not reside in the World of Spirits but do reside in heaven or the Celestial Kingdom. Joseph Smith describes these just men when he taught,

> *There are **two kinds of beings in heaven**-viz., angels, who are resurrected personages, having bodies of flesh and bones. 2nd. The spirits of just men made perfect- they who are not resurrected, but inherit the same glory.*[225]

And further the Lord taught,

> *These are they who are just men made perfect through Jesus the mediator of the new covenant, who wrought out this perfect atonement **through the shedding of his own blood**.* [226]

There are two points to be understood by these scriptures.

---

[223] Matthew 27:52-53
[224] D&C 138:57
[225] Smith, History of the Church, 5:267, See also D&C 129:1-3
[226] D&C 76:69

1. If a person is martyred because of their testifying of the Savior, they become perfect through the Savior's atonement because they gave their ultimate sacrifice for the cause of the Savior. They did not deny him.
2. After their death, they reside not in the World of Spirits as described above but in heaven with other perfected people until their resurrection.

Some righteous men who achieved perfection by their dedication to the will of the Father would also be with the *"just men made perfect."* in heaven. Noah also known as Gabriel and Elias are such men. Noah was not martyred. But Noah, identified as Gabriel, appeared to Mary to announce that she would bear the Son of God. This event is recorded as

*And in the sixth month the **angel Gabriel was sent from God** unto a city of Galilee, named Nazareth,*

To a virgin espoused to a man whose name was Joseph, of the house of David; and the virgin's name was Mary."[227]

Gabriel (Noah) then announced that Mary would bear the Son of God and told her of her mission. It should be noted that Joseph Smith identified Gabriel as Noah.[228] He came from the presence of God.

The angel that appeared to Zacharias, the father of John the Baptist, is recorded in Luke as Gabriel. The Lord states in a latter-day revelation that it was the prophet Elias and not Gabriel[229] that appeared to Zacharias. Elias stated that he stood,

In the presence of God; and am sent to speak unto thee, and to shew thee these glad tidings" [230]

President Joseph F. Smith specifically mentions that Noah[231] and Elias[232] were two of those in attendance at the Savior's coming to the world of spirits.

---

[227] Luke 1:26-27
[228] Smith, History of the Church 3:385
[229] D&C 27::6-7
[230] Luke 1:19
[231] D&C 138:41
[232] D&C 138:45

There is one other group that is in this group with "Just Men Made Perfect." Alma and Amulek had converts in Ammonihah. They were driven out of Ammonihah by men who were to cast stones at them.

The wives and children of these Ammonihah converts were burned along with their records by the Ammonihah leaders. As they were being burned up with their records, Alma declined taking action to save them and spoke to Amulek,

> *the Lord receiveth them up unto himself, in glory*

These women and children were being received by the Lord himself which would place them with other perfect people in his presence. They would be the same as "Just men made perfect" having given their lives for the Savior.

Little Children

The atonement of the Savior provides that little children do not become subject to Satan,

> *But behold, I say unto you, that little children are redeemed from the foundation of the world through mine Only Begotten;*
>
> *Wherefore, they cannot sin, for power is not given unto Satan to tempt little children, until they begin to become accountable before me;*[233]

And also,

> *Listen to the words of Christ, your Redeemer, your Lord and your God. Behold, I came into the world not to call the righteous but sinners to repentance; the whole need no physician, but they that are sick; wherefore, little children are whole, for they are not capable of committing sin; wherefore the curse of Adam is taken from them in me,*[234]

These statements have significance for those children who die in their infancy up to the age of accountability which is eight years old. These children are pure and will be in the presence of the Father and Savior. Older children will be accountable according to the teachings of their

---

[233] D&C 29:46-47
[234] Moroni 8:8

parents. If the parent's teachings were righteous and the child rebelled, the child will be responsible for his/her own actions.

However, it is expected that many would be found worthy to be raised in righteousness when they are resurrected and be worthy of eternal life.

Joseph F. Smith was about 6 years old when his father, Hyrum and Joseph were martyred. As he grew older, he became aware of the following story about his father,

> *Bishop Edward Hunter's son (who died when a little child) came to him, in the stature of full-grown manhood, and revealed himself to his father, and said: 'I am your son.'*
>
> *Bishop Hunter did not understand it. He went to my father and said: 'Hyrum, what does that mean? I buried my son when he was only a little boy, but he has come to me as a full-grown man—a noble, glorious, young man, and declared himself my son. What does it mean?'*
>
> *Father (Hyrum Smith, the Patriarch) told him that <u>the Spirit of Jesus Christ was full-grown before he was born into the world; and so our children were full-grown and possessed their full stature in the spirit, before they entered mortality, the same stature that they will possess after they have passed away from mortality</u>, and as they will also appear after the resurrection, when they shall have completed their mission.*
>
> *Joseph Smith taught the doctrine* **that the infant child that was laid away in death would come up in the resurrection as a child;** *and, pointing to the mother of a lifeless child, he said to her:* **'You will have the joy, the pleasure, and satisfaction of nurturing this child, after its resurrection, until it reaches the full stature of its spirit.**'[235]

In 1854 Joseph met his aunt, Agnes, the wife of Don Carlos, brother to Joseph Smith and during their conversation she told Joseph F Smith that at the funeral of her daughter, Sophronia, that the prophet was speaking at the funeral and told her,

---

[235] Gospel Doctrine, p 455

> *She should have **the joy, the pleasure and the satisfaction of rearing that child, after the resurrection, until it reached the full stature of its spirit;** and that <u>it would be a far greater joy than she could possible have in mortality, because she would be free from the sorrow and the fear and the disabilities of mortal life, and that she would know more than she could know in this life.</u>*[236]

Joseph F. Smith then stated that Agnes bore her testimony to him that what she described was absolutely true. A little later he conversed with Lorin Walker, husband of his oldest sister, who was at this same funeral and he confirmed what his aunt Agnes had said. Joseph F. asked Lorin what Joseph had said about little children. He responded,

> *The body remains undeveloped in the grave, but the spirit returns to God who gave it. Afterwards, in the resurrection, the spirit and the body will be reunited; the body will develop and grow to the full stature of the spirit; and the resurrected soul will go on to perfection,*[237]

Following that, Joseph F talked with M. Isabelle Horne who attended this same funeral with her husband. She confirmed everything he had previously heard. She and her husband gave Joseph F. Smith an affidavit stating what she and her husband had heard. Their statement stated that little children will be resurrected and grow to the maturity of their spirit and this was declared by Joseph Smith.

Then Joseph heard Franklin D. Richards, who spoke of this incident in public. Joseph then went to President Woodruff and Cannon and explained what he had collected. They approved as doctrine taught by Joseph Smith that the concept of those dying in childhood would be resurrected in the same stature as when they died. They would grow to the full stature of their spirit and go on to perfection. After this approval, Joseph F. Smith began to teach this doctrine in his talks.[238]

About 2 ½ months prior to his martyrdom, Joseph Smith is quoted as saying the following about the resurrection of children,

> *A question will Mothers have their children in Eternity yes, yes, you will have the children But as it falls so it will rise, It will*

---

[236] Gospel Doctrine, p 456

[237] Gospel Doctrine, P 456

[238] Gospel Doctrine, P 456-457

never grow, It will be in its precise form as it fell in its mothers arms.

Eternity is full of thrones upon which dwell thousands of children reigning on thrones of glory <u>not one cubit added to their stature</u>.[239]

Joseph Smith has stated many times that at the resurrection, every person who is resurrected will be resurrected in the same stature as when they died. Babies will be resurrected as babies, adults resurrected as adults.

The second paragraph of this quote identifies an inconsistent statement with what he told Agnes. This is not the only record that Joseph has stated that resurrected children will not grow following their resurrection. The question is how do we explain Joseph Smith's different statements.

Joseph recognized he was not a perfect man. He told a group of newly arrived brothers and sisters at the red brick store in Nauvoo,

> *I told them that I was but a man, and they must not expect me to be perfect; if they expected perfection from me, I should expect it from them;*[240]

On the 12 May 1844, Thomas Bullock recorded Joseph saying,

> *I never told you that I was perfect-but there is no error in the revelations which I have taught*[241]

Further research on FamilyHistory.org identifies that Agnes's husband, Don Carlos Smith, died on 7 Aug 1841. So, at the time of her daughter's funeral, Agnes was deeply grieving for the loss of her daughter and her husband. Joseph was inspired by the Savior to say what he said to give Agnes peace and understanding, which she so deeply needed. His statement to Agnes was revelation; but not recorded by him and taught as such.

---

[239] Words of Joseph smith, p 347 recorded-Wilford Woodruff; 7 April 1844
[240] The words of Joseph Smith, p. 132
[241] The words of Joseph Smith, p. 369

Children Resurrection

The reason that Agnes was told that she would raise her daughter after their resurrection is that her daughter had not developed enough in mortality to be blessed in eternity. There was more knowledge and understanding that she needed to be taught. Once she has that knowledge, she could then go on to perfection. She will need to have the temple ordinances completed for herself, identify a companion for eternity, and be married in the temple by proxy by proper authority. When these things are done, she will be qualified for eternal life. Dying young guarantees little children, a pathway to eternal life and exaltation.

All babies and children who die before their age of accountability will have to be resurrected in the same form as when they died. Then they will have "parents" raise them to their physical growth potential so that their physical bodies will have the same stature as their spirit body. Regardless of what culture their mortal parents were, they will have "parents" assigned to raise them, be they uncles or aunts or grandparents who are worthy to raise them.

These activities will be done during the millennium. There are no resurrections occurring at the present time. The next resurrection will be the massive resurrections of the faithful to meet the Savior, when he comes to usher in the millennium. This resurrection will include the "converts" that have accepted the gospel that is preached to them in the world of spirits.

Righteous Adults following this resurrection will act as "parents" to babies and little children that will be resurrected during the millennium. Babies will need to be held, fed, cuddled and taught as they develop. They need to develop so that they are prepared to receive the temple ordinances by proxy. They will need to identify a companion to be married for time and eternity also by proxy. Then they will have eternal life. The Savior will be on the earth to manage all of the processes and procedures that will be used. As Joseph Smith stated,

> *Eternity is full of thrones upon which dwell thousands of children reigning on thrones of glory.*[242]

---

[242] Words of Joseph smith, p 347 recorded-Wilford Woodruff; 7 April 1844

These children are prepared from their resurrection by their "parents" until they are fully qualified to be on those thrones.

ANGER – PERFECTION

One of the most challenging and misunderstood events was the Savior cleansing the temple. It is misunderstood because many people conclude and believe the Savior in his anger used strong force to remove the polluters from the temple. Many paintings depict the Savior with raised arm with whip in hand standing in majesty above cowering men.

Many terrible acts have been committed by persons who are angry. This book will address anger in general terms and then address the cleansing of the temple as it relates to the Savior's perfection.

Consulting several dictionaries, anger or being angry is defined as,

> *a **strong feeling** of displeasure and belligerence aroused by a wrong.* [243]

The wrong in this definition could be a perceived wrong and not an actual fact. Anger must be strong and belligerent. A feeling of displeasure is not anger.

The difference between feeling displeasure and anger is the intensity with which the emotion is felt. Anger is an emotion that can cause people to lose self-control and consequently cause great misery, injury, damage, destruction and even death.

Tool of Satan

There are a number of examples from the scriptures of how Satan uses anger to accomplish his purposes. In the Book of Mormon, Ammon and his brethren traveled to the Lamanites to teach and convert as many as they possibly could. King Lamoni and a number of his people were converted. They became known as the people of Anti-Nephi-Lehi.

The Amalekites appear to be a group of Nephites that developed a deep hatred against their culture and were living among the Lamanites. This conclusion is drawn from the fact that the Amalekites and the Ammonites, were largely of the religion called

---

[243] http://dictionary.reference.com/browse/anger?s=t Last visited July 2020

the "Nehors." This religion was practiced among the Nephites and they were identified separately from the Lamanites as opposed to being included as Lamanites.[244]

In one event the Amalekites having a hatred of the Nephites stirred up the Lamanites to go to war against the Nephites. The Amalekites and Lamanites were defeated in battle. After their defeat they redirected their anger against the Anti-Nephi-Lehi people for a second time. On the first occasion the Anti-Nephi-Lehi people did not resist and many were killed, but the Lamanites stopped the killing and many Lamanite converts were made. On this occasion they were advised differently,

> *And it came to pass that the Amalekites, because of their loss, were exceedingly angry. And when they saw that they could not seek revenge from the Nephites,* ***they began to stir up the people in anger against their brethren, the people of Anti-Nephi-Lehi; therefore they began again to destroy them.*** [245]

Ammon petitioned the Lord to determine whether King Limhi and his people, known as the people of Anti-Nephi-Lehi, should go with Ammon and return to Zarahemla or not. The Lord responded,

> *Get this people out of this land, that they perish not; for* ***Satan has great hold on the hearts of the Amalekites,*** <u>***who do stir up the Lamanites to anger***</u> ***against their brethren to slay them*** *... and blessed are this people in this generation, for I will preserve them.* [246]

Another example of Satan's power to influence people to anger is described in Mormons letter to his son, Moroni, describing the Nephites of his time,

> *And now behold, my son, I fear lest the Lamanites shall destroy these people; for they do not repent, and* ***Satan stirreth them up continually to anger one with another.***
>
> *Behold, I am laboring with them continually; and* ***when I speak the word of God with sharpness they tremble and anger against me***; *and when I use no sharpness they harden their hearts against*

---

[244] Alma 21:2-5
[245] Alma 27:2.
[246] Alma 27:12.

it; wherefore, *I fear lest the Spirit of the Lord hath ceased striving with them.* [247]

When Mormon presses his people to change their ways, they respond with anger and never change. Eventually they were destroyed by the Lamanites.

The Lord had this to say about the people who stole the 117 pages of manuscript of the first translation of the Book of Mormon,

> *For, behold, they shall not accomplish their evil designs in lying against those words. For, behold, if you should bring forth the same words they will say that you have lied and that you have pretended to translate, but that you have contradicted yourself.*
>
> *And, behold,* **they will publish this, and Satan will harden the hearts of the people to stir them up to anger against you, that they will not believe my words.** [248]

The Lord did not have Joseph retranslate that part which was taken but substituted the translation of the small plates of Nephi to replace that which was lost. Consequently, those who made the changes were prevented from causing anger against the Prophet.

In speaking of purchasing lands in Zion the Lord said,

> *Wherefore, I the Lord will that you should purchase the lands, that you may have advantage of the world, that you may have claim on the world,* ***that they may not be stirred up unto anger.***
>
> ***For Satan putteth it into their hearts to anger against you, and to the shedding of blood.*** [249]

The Savior taught in the Sermon on the Mount and also to the Nephites the following about anger,

> *But I say unto you, that* ***whoswever is angry with his brother shall be in danger of his judgment,*** [250]

---

[247] Moroni 9:3-4
[248] D&C 10:31-32
[249] D&C 63:27-28
[250] 3 Nephi 12:21–22, Matthew 5:20-21

The Savior said this about anger to the Nephites when he appeared to them,

> *Behold, this is **not my doctrine, to stir up the hearts of men with anger**, one against another; but this is <u>my doctrine, that such things should be done away</u>.* [251]

Anger is a tool of Satan.

Nephi's Anger

Nephi's anger with his brothers Laman and Lemuel is a good example of how anger interferes with having the spirit of the Lord. This is illustrated in Nephi's psalm.[252] Most people are puzzled by the depth of despair and the sins described by Nephi. Some use it as a justification that if so great a prophet as Nephi has great sins, they are not so bad off with their sins. In order to understand Nephi's psalm, we need to understand his situation at the time of his writing. This writing occurred right after his father's death. He recorded,

> *And it came to pass after my father, Lehi, had spoken unto all his household, according to the feelings of his heart and the Spirit of the Lord which was in him, he waxed old. And it came to pass that he died, and was buried.*
>
> *And it came to pass that **not many days after his death, Laman and Lemuel and the sons of Ishmael were angry with me** because of the admonitions of the Lord.*
>
> *For I, Nephi, was constrained to speak unto them, according to his word; for I had spoken many things unto them, and also my father, before his death; many of which sayings are written upon mine other plates.*[253]

While Lehi was alive, he was a measure of protection to Nephi. By their Jewish custom, sons needed to obey their father although Laman and Lemuel did rebel against their father at times. Although they obeyed their father by leaving Jerusalem with him, they complained

---

[251] 3 Nephi 11:30

[252] 2 Nephi 4:17-35

[253] 2 Nephi 4:12-14

bitterly and even threatened Nephi's death at times. Nephi further recorded after his father's death,

> *Behold, it came to pass that I, Nephi, did cry much unto the Lord my God, because of the anger of my brethren.*
>
> *But behold,* **their anger did increase against me, insomuch that they did seek to take away my life.**
>
> *Yea, they did murmur against me, saying: Our younger brother thinks to rule over us; and we have had much trial because of him; wherefore, now let us slay him, that we may not be afflicted more because of his words. For behold, we will not have him to be our ruler; for it belongs unto us, who are the elder brethren, to rule over this people.*[254]

Nephi was the object of Laman and Lemuel hatred to the point of wanting to kill him. We will now turn to Nephi's psalm to understand his feelings. He wrote,

> *O wretched man that I am! Yea, my heart sorroweth because of my flesh; my soul grieved because of mine iniquities.* [255]

Nephi then recounts many dreams, visitations of angels, mercies and visions some of which he was commanded not to write. Then he says,

> *And why should I yield to sin, because of my flesh? Yea, why should I give way to temptations, <u>that the evil one have placed in my heart to destroy my peace</u> and afflict my soul?* **Why am I angry because of my enemy?** [256]

Nephi was angry with his enemy! And who was his enemy? His enemy was his brothers Laman and Lemuel who wanted to kill him. In fact, Nephi referred to his brothers and those that followed them as his enemy or enemies some seven (7) times during his psalm.[257] He never spoke of them as his brothers. They were always spoken of as enemies.

He had been in control of his emotions and forgiving them throughout their trials in arriving at the promised land. At this time,

---

[254] 2 Nephi 5:1-3
[255] 2 Nephi 4:17
[256] 2 Nephi 4:27
[257] 2 Nephi 4:22, 27-29, 31, 33

Nephi's emotional response was that he was very angry with his brothers because he had been so patient with their past angry challenges, even threatening his life. He had been so forgiving and his brothers paid no attention to past events.

We need to address the expression which is quoted above,

> Yea, why should I give way to temptations, <u>that the evil one have place in my heart to destroy my peace</u> and afflict my soul?

In this expression, he speaks of an "*evil one*" having a place "*in his heart.*" What Nephi was feeling was anger, a tool of Satan. Nephi knows that feeling anger is wrong and destroys his peace. He further writes of his solution or of his repentance:

> *Awake, my soul! No longer droop in sin. Rejoice, O my heart, and give place no more for the **enemy of my soul**.*
>
> *Do not **anger again because of mine enemies**.*[258]

And what was the "enemy of my soul"? It was his anger! It was destroying Nephi's peace. Notice that Nephi again refers to his brothers as his enemy and not his brethren. This describes what has happened to his relationship with his brothers. Nephi's solution, or repentance, was "Do not anger again." He knows he has to control this anger by eliminating it.

Nephi wrote so negatively about his anger calling it his sins. In the beginning verses Nephi was lamenting his sin but talked about it in the plural, sins. This is what is generally confusing to readers. His writing sounds like he has committed many serious sins but he has only one. Nephi lamented his anger because it was destroying his peace and his ability to have the spirit of God with him. This would prevent any more visions, dreams or communications from God until it was removed.

This was a huge challenge to Nephi. After Lehi died and was buried, Nephi gave counsel to his brothers and they rejected his teachings. They took the position that they were the elder sons and the leadership belonged to them by right of seniority and custom in spite of an angel telling them differently[259]. They completely ignored the

---

[258] 2 Nephi 4:28-29
[259] 1 Nephi 3:29

angel's message to them that Nephi would be their leader. They no longer followed Nephi's leadership and counsel and wanted to kill him.[260] Nephi's reaction in this case was anger. In all the offenses that Laman and Lemuel committed against Nephi, this was the first time that Nephi was angry with his brothers. He had been so long-suffering and patient and put forth a great deal of effort to help his brothers to be righteous. But they would have none of it.

There were five major incidents[261] where Laman and Lemuel were angry with Nephi (and Sam). In all cases Nephi was full of the spirit, patient and concerned about his brothers. He had no anger. Note how angry the brothers were in each situation. They acted on that anger in each situation and threatened Nephi with death except for the first instance when they beat Nephi and Sam. They sinned because of their anger and were brought to repentance by various means in every case.

But this last time was different. Their father, Lehi, had died. Laman and Lemuel's attempts to kill Nephi were increasing and more serious. Shortly after this Nephi was inspired to separate from his brothers, which he did. The one lesson that we should learn from Nephi's experience is that the spirit and peace of God cannot dwell in a person who is angry. If you have anger in your heart it interferes with the spirit or Holy Ghost and his potential communications.

Savior's Anger?

Did the Savior exercise anger during his earthly ministry? There are two things that need to be addressed. One is a scripture and the other is the temple cleansing.

The Savior entered a synagogue on the Sabbath day. A man with a withered hand was there. Pharisees were also there to see if the Savior would heal the man on the Sabbath day,

And he saith unto them, Is it lawful to do good on the sabbath days, or to do evil? to save life, or to kill? But they held their peace.

---

[260] 2 Nephi 4:13-14, 2 Nephi 5:1-4
[261] 1 Nephi 3:28-30, 7:7-21, 16:34-39, 17:7-55, 18:10-20

*And when he had looked round about on them **with anger, being grieved** for the hardness of their hearts, he saith unto the man, Stretch forth thine hand. And he stretched it out: and his hand was restored whole as the other.* [262]

This scripture is not accurate. The Savior would have no anger when at the same time he healed and blessed the man with making his hand whole. He had no anger! His love prevailed.

John' Temple Cleansing

John records that Jesus,

found in the temple those that sold oxen and sheep and doves, and the changers of money sitting:

And when he had made a scourge of small cords, he drove them all out of the temple, and the sheep, and the oxen; and poured out the changers' money, and overthrew the tables;

And said unto them that sold doves, Take these things hence; make not my Father's house an house of merchandise. [263]

This scene is view by many as the Savior going up to those in the temple swinging his hand made scourge and whipping the polluters to drive them out. This is illustrated by artists works which can be viewed on the internet.[264] Many of these paintings depict cowering men with the Savior's arm raised ready to strike with his scourge. This is suggested by John's record that the Savior made a scourge and then drove them out. This is not an accurate understanding. John writes that the Savior drove them out of the temple and then told some to leave which is an inconsistent statement. How could he tell them to leave when they were already out?

John's record shows the Savior,

- made a scourge,
- drove out the sheep and the oxen,
- poured out the changers' money,
- overthrew the tables,

---

[262] Mark 3:4-5

[263] John 2:14-16

[264] Using Bing or other search engine; Enter "pictures Jesus cleansing temple"

- told the dove owners to remove their doves,

This list does not specifically show the order or how the events developed. First of all, we need to understand that the Savior would not just walk in and start swinging the scourge and demanding that they leave. He would never do that! This is not compatible with the Savior's character as demonstrated in other New Testament events. Also, it is not compatible with the Father's refusal to accept Satan's plan of using force to make us live gospel principles.

The Savior would not do anything until he gave the polluters an opportunity to correct their sinful conduct. His ministry clearly demonstrates that he did not use physical force in any of his other activities.

The Savior's mission was to teach, minister and not judge except for his judgment of Jewish leaders. The Savior's purpose was to get those who polluted the temple, out so that he could teach the temple ordinances and other gospel principles, minister and heal in this sacred place. He had a firmness of purpose and he needed to have these polluters gone.

This description that follows is the likely course of events. When the Savior first entered the temple with his scourge, he would have told the money changers and those that bought and sold the oxen and sheep that they would have to leave and that they were polluting his Father's house. The scourge would be at this side.

They would be surprised because they were not accustomed to hear that kind of command. Holding true to their charge they would probably refuse to obey thinking that no one should give them such a command except the Chief Priest who ran the temple. Who was this man telling them to leave? Strong language probably followed.

To demonstrate his firmness of purpose, the Savior would then turn over the table which scattered the money. He would tell them more firmly that they were polluting his Father's house and to take their money and leave. Then he would turn to the dove sellers and tell them that they were polluting the temple and to leave. While the money changers and the sellers were picking up their money, he would use his whip to drive the oxen and sheep out of the temple grounds.

There is a painting by William Brassey Hole, 1846-1917 that illustrates this scene. He painted many Bible scenes, of which 80 watercolor pictures were displayed in a book entitled "Life of Jesus of Nazareth." From his study and work, he came to understand the character of the Savior. This picture is a copy of one of his paintings.

Notice the table being picked up by one person and a second person picking up money, with the Savor pointing the way to leave the temple. His right arm is at his side holding the whip and is not active. The animals were in the background to be driven out by the Savior. On his way to drive out the cattle and sheep, the dove owners would pack up believing that he might open their cages and let the doves out.

This would be a startling event to these polluters. These people had never been challenged in this manner. Once the polluters had gathered their money they would leave, having no purpose to remain. Their merchandise, the oxen and sheep, were out of the temple. They were out of business with the animals gone. The sellers of doves would take their doves out of the temple with them fearing that the Savior would open their cages and let the doves escape as they witnessed him driving out the oxen and sheep.

The Savior did no physical harm or damage to the men personally. He did not use the whip on the men. After the cattle and sheep were driven out, the men would leave having nothing to sell.

This author believes that his displeasure did not rise to the level of anger as we mortals know it. After the polluters were gone the Savior taught, blessed and healed in the temple. He taught of the sacredness of the temple and the sacred ordinances that belong therein. It was his purpose to restore these things by fulfilling the Law of Moses and restoring all that had been taken away at the time the Law of Moses was taught.

James E Talmage View

James E. Talmage wrote of the temple cleansings. In his book, Jesus the Christ, Talmage made this statement describing John's temple cleansing,

> *Three years before, at Passover time,* **He had been wrought up to a high state of righteous anger** *by a similar exhibition of sordid chaffering within the sacred precincts, and had driven out the sheep and oxen, and* **forcibly expelled the traders and the money-changers and all who were using** *His Father's house as a house of merchandise.*[265]

This is the response that most people have because they read that Jesus made a scourge and then drove them all out. The assumption is that the scourge was used as the tool to drive the people out. That kind of action would reflect deep anger.

Talmage used this phrase "righteous anger" to describe the Savior's actions. Talmage thought that the Savior used the whip on men as most view this scene. He coined the term "righteous anger" because he knew that the Savior had not sinned and he visualized the Savior as having intensive anger because they were polluting his father's house. Also, there are many scriptures that describe the anger of God. So, his anger was righteous. He did not take into account the many scriptures that show that anger is a tool of Satan. In viewing the scene as described above, that anger is missing.

---

[265] Talmage, Jesus the Christ 490

To Nephi his anger was an enemy to his soul and prevented him from having the spirit with him. His anger was sinful. To say that the Savior was angry, a tool of Satan, in the same way would make the Savior sinful and not our example.

TEMPLE CLEANSING

There have been ongoing discussions in our Church and in Christianity as to whether there were two events where the temple was cleansed or was there only one. This book makes the case that only one temple cleansing happened.

Temple Ordinance Status

We need to understand what the Savior's primary motivation or purpose was for cleansing the temple. It is not enough to understand that the temple was held in high esteem by the Savior and the Jewish people. There was more to the Savior's mission than just teaching and healing in the temple.

Today we understand that our primary goals should be to be "*married in the temple for time and all eternity*" and "*endure to the end.*" Family is the primary unit in eternity. But what was the temple ordinance status at the time the Savior was born?

The Levites were ministering in the temple with ordinances having their roots from Moses. These Levites exercised the Aaronic or Levitical priesthood. The general male population **could not become Melchizedek Priesthood holders** which is necessary to receive the temple ordinances. In addition, the sealing keys were taken from the earth by Elijah (9th century BC) when he was taken from the earth in a chariot. Following this no one could be married for time and all eternity. No one held the keys on earth. Even the prophets of the old testament or the Nephite prophets of the Book of Mormon, could not be married for time and all eternity. There were no "*keys*" held by anyone on earth following Elijah.

The Savior needed to restore these keys and teach the apostles the temple ordinances. This was absolutely necessary so that Israel and converts to the Savior's gospel could qualify for the temple ordinances. This was absolutely necessary for the eternal salvation of these people.

The events on the Mount of Transfiguration were pivotal in preparation for the Savior restoring the temple ordinances. The Mount of Transfiguration did not occur at the beginning of his ministry. It appears that it took place towards the end of the third year of his ministry.

Willard Richards had a document which is identified as his pocket companion which contained teachings by Joseph Smith. In the document it states that Adam was given the keys of the Priesthood. Then it states,

> *The priesthood is everlasting. The Savior, Moses and Elias – gave the Keys to Peter, James and John on the Mount when they were transfigured before him*[266].

Some in the Church have taught that Elias was really Elijah. However, in Joseph F. Smith's revelation he identified the prophet Elias, as being present with Moses[267] on the Mount of Transfiguration.

So, from the preceding quote, the Savior, Moses and Elias each gave keys they possessed to Peter, James and John on the Mount of Transfiguration. The Savior's keys were the governing keys of the priesthood, which includes the temple sealing keys held by Elijah. These were the keys necessary to perform valid temple ordinances. Elijah was not present because the Savior was present and gave those keys to Peter, James and John.

Remember that this event on the Mount of Transfiguration did not happen until later in the Savior's ministry. Please note that all members of the Presidency, Peter, James and John, were given those keys. The restoration of the keys by the Savior was necessary prior to the actual temple ordinances being taught to the apostles. After receiving the keys and then being taught the ordinances, the apostles could then minister to the people these important ordinances in the temple.

Again, we emphasize that these keys were not given to Peter, James and John until later in the Savior's ministry. So, cleaning of the temple at the beginning of the Savior's ministry did not happen.

---

[266] Ehat, Words of Joseph Smith, 9
[267] D&C 138:45

When the temple was cleansed at the end of the Savior's ministry, it created an environment where the Savior could teach the actual temple ordinances to the apostles in addition to other teachings and blessings he performed. The apostles could then teach temple ordinances to Jewish and gentile converts.

Luke records,

> *And they, continuing daily with one accord in the temple, and breaking bread from house to house, did eat their meat with gladness and singleness of heart,*[268]

For a short time, it seems they would have educated and performed the ordinances in the temple until they were excluded from using the temple by the governing priests. Then other places were designated as places where the temple ordinances could be performed.

One Cleansing

The restoring of the temple ordinances prior to his crucifixion was necessary for the saints following Christ to enjoy the same temple blessings that we enjoy today. The Book of John identifies a cleansing event as occurring at the very beginning of the Savior's ministry.

The Gospel of John has no wording that would give us a clue as to the purpose of cleansing the temple at this early date. It is doubtful that the Apostles were called to be apostles at the time of the first cleansing. Certainly, no priesthood keys had been given to Peter, James and John by this time. What then was the reason for cleansing the temple at this early time? There is none! It did not happen.

If the temple were cleansed at this early date it was polluted again soon thereafter. It would have to be cleansed again in three years to accomplish the temple education that needed to be done. To cleanse the temple, then leave to minister to the people for three years letting it be polluted again does not make sense. Nothing of value could be accomplished at the time of this first claimed cleansing.

---

[268] Acts 2:46, See also 5:17-21; 25

Cleansing the temple at the end of his ministry allowed him to teach, heal and minister to the people and to complete the restoration of the temple ordinances.

Savior's Challenge

There is one more major point that should be made to show the first temple cleansing did not happen. Following the first cleansing of the temple as recorded in John, the Jewish leadership questioned his authority to do the things that he did,

> *Jesus answered and said unto them, Destroy this temple, and in three days I will raise it up.*
>
> *Then said the Jews,* **Forty and six years was this temple in building, and wilt thou rear it up in three days?**
>
> *But he spake of the temple of his body.* [269]

What the Savior said was "Destroy my body and I will live again in three days." Why would he say that to the Jewish leadership when he was not ready to be crucified and resurrected? He would only say this statement if he was prepared to end his life. This quote from John was said at the end of his ministry, not the beginning.

SINS OF THE WORLD

When the Savior appeared to the Nephites the first words uttered to them were:

> *Behold, I am Jesus Christ, whom the prophets testified shall come into the world.*
>
> *And behold, I am the light and the life of the world; and I have drunk out of that bitter cup which the Father hath given me, and* **have glorified the Father in taking upon me the sins of the world***, in the which I have suffered the will of the Father*[270] *in all things from the beginning.*[271]

And further he demonstrated his resurrection,

---

[269] John 2:18-21

[270] The reason for the title of this book.

[271] 3 Nephi 11:11

> *Arise and come forth unto me, that ye may thrust your hands into my side, and also that ye may feel the prints of the nails in my hands and in my feet, **that ye may know that I am the God of Israel, and the God of the whole earth**, and have been **slain for the sins of the world**.* [272]

The Savior verifies that he is the "*God of Israel and the God of the whole earth.*" By feeling the scarred wounds in his hands, feet and side these Nephites would know who he was. He also states that he was "*slain for the sins of the world*" and by so doing has taken "*upon me the sins of the world.*"

This expression "sins of the world" has a broader concept than his judgments for individual sin. When the Savior makes judgments regarding individual sins, he is judging individual people for qualifications for their eternal station, which are,

- ➢ Celestial Kingdom - Highest Degree
- ➢ Terrestrial Kingdom
- ➢ Telestial Kingdom
- ➢ Outer Darkness

There are eight (8) scriptures that say that Christ was "slain" or crucified for the "sins of the world."[273] There are nine (9) others that say that Christ will take away, atone for or bear the "sins of the world" or that Christ will take upon him the "sins of the world."[274] To take away, atone for, bear or take upon him the sins of the world means that the Savior is responsible to the Father to provide the resurrection for all and a salvation of some kind for all of Father's children according to the plan we accepted before the world was.

The one exception is those who become sons of perdition. They will receive no salvation. However, the Savior will be responsible to see that the sons of perdition eventually will be placed where they will not have power or influence on the rest of Father's children throughout eternity.

---

[272] 3 Nephi 11:14
[273] D&C 76:40–44, 1 Nephi 11:33, Alma 30:26, D&C 21:9, D&C 35:2, D&C 46:13, D&C 53:2, D&C 54:1
[274] 1 Nephi 10:10; Alma 5:48, 7:13, 34:8, 36:17, 42:12; Mosiah 26:23;

We commonly understand that all who are not sons of perdition will be consigned to the Celestial Kingdom, Terrestrial Kingdom or the Telestial Kingdom[275].

A voice declared to Joseph Smith and Sidney Rigdon in their revelation of the kingdoms of glory about the full mission of the Savior,

> *And this is the gospel, the glad tidings, which the voice out of the heavens bore record unto us*
>
> *That he came into the world, even* **Jesus, to be crucified for the world, and to bear the sins of the world, and <u>to sanctify the world, and to cleanse it from all unrighteousness;</u>**
>
> **That through him all might be saved whom the Father had put into his power and made by him;**
>
> <u>**Who glorifies the Father, and saves all the works of his hands, except those sons of perdition who deny the Son after the Father has revealed him.**</u> [276]

This scripture verifies that his atonement is to provide a salvation of some kind for all who are not sons of perdition. He further states that his purpose is to "*sanctify the world and to cleanse it from all unrighteousness.*" To sanctify the world means to make the earth holy. This earth will be made holy to become a Celestial world and the place where those worthy of being in the Celestial Kingdom will dwell. This cleansing will occur by eliminating all unrighteous beings or things from it. The Savior made a covenant with the church members in which he said,

> *And this shall be my covenant with you, ye shall have it for the land of your inheritance, and for the inheritance of your children forever, while the earth shall stand, and* **ye shall possess it again in eternity, no more to pass away.** [277]

This scripture establishes that worthy members of the Church will inhabit the earth in eternity. But those of the Telestial and Terrestrial Kingdoms do not have this promise and will not be on the earth.

---

[275] D&C 76
[276] D&C 76:39–43
[277] D&C 38:20

Eventually the earth is only for those worthy of the Celestial Kingdom as determined in Christ's teachings.

It is well established that the resurrection of all will be the reuniting of our physical bodies with our spirits. Since our resurrected bodies are physical there must be a physical place for these physical bodies to reside. Nothing has been revealed about where these other kingdoms will be. Since the Savior has taken upon him the "sins of the world" he is responsible to provide the places where these other kingdoms will be located. Those people in the Telestial Kingdom will be:

> *as innumerable as the stars in the firmament of heaven, or as the sand upon the seashore.* [278]

Whatever planet or physical place the Savior will provide must be very large to accommodate this group

Kingdoms, Dominions and Glory

During the final preparations for the Savior to complete his atonement he said to his apostles,

> *In my Father's house are many mansions: if it were not so, I would have told you. I go to prepare a place for you.*[279]

Joseph Smith in explaining this scripture said,

> *My text is on the resurrection of the dead, which you will find in the 14th chapter of John- 'In my Father's house are many mansions. It should be-'In my Father's kingdom are many kingdoms,' in order that ye may be heirs of God and joint-heirs with me.*[280]

Here Joseph is saying that the Savior's statement is referring to kingdoms in the highest degree of the Celestial Kingdom. Those who inherit the highest degree in the Celestial Kingdom will have a Kingdom and are priests/priestesses and kings/queens[281] and will

---

[278] D&C 76:109

[279] John `14:2

[280] Quote from History of the Church. Citation lost and could not be found.

[281] D&C 76:56

dwell in the presence of the Father and Christ[282]. There are many kingdoms in the Celestial Kingdom each ruled by a king.

These are equal in power, might and dominion[283]. Notice that glory is not mentioned in this list. The glory of individuals in the Celestial Kingdom will be different but will grow as worlds are created, inhabited and made Celestial. Those who inherit the Celestial Kingdom will receive glory in the same way as our Father. His glory grows when some of his children qualify to be with him in the Celestial Kingdom.

Joseph further said this about mansions:

*There are mansions for those who obey a celestial law, and **there are other mansions for those who come short of the law, every man in his own order.*** [284]

The question is: "What are these mansions of which Joseph spoke?" According to Section 76 all individuals in the Terrestrial and Telestial Kingdoms will have a "dominion."[285] The term dominion as defined in dictionaries refers to ruling power, authority or control. Joseph was referring to these dominions as mansions. Each person will have a mansion or dominion "*in his own order.*" These scriptures indicate that each person will have a glory related to that mansion.

How does glory relate to these dominions? A scripture relating to Telestial inhabitants gives us a clue to this question. Each person in the Telestial Kingdom will have his own dominion. The scriptures record the following quote of those in the Telestial Kingdom,

*And the glory of the telestial is one, even as the glory of the stars is one; **for as one star differs from another star in glory, even so differs one from another in glory in the telestial world.*** [286]

And continuing about those in the Telestial Kingdom,

---

[282] D&C 76:62

[283] D&C 76:95

[284] Smith, History of the Church Vol 6, P 365

[285] D&C 76:95, 91, 111

[286] D&C 76:98

*For they shall be judged according to their works, and every man shall receive according to his own works, his **own dominion, in the mansions which are prepared***[287]

So, each person in the Telestial Kingdom will have a dominion and a glory which will be dependent on the good works they perform in mortality. All souls are not equal in the Telestial Kingdom. This principle is often overlooked. A further note of those in the Telestial Kingdom is:

*And **they shall be servants of the Most High**; but where God and Christ dwell they cannot come, worlds without end.* [288]

Being a servant during mortality is far different than being a servant to the Father in eternity which will never change. They will always be servants doing the Father's bidding managing the dominion that they will receive. They can never go to be with the Father.

What about those in the Terrestrial Kingdom? Joseph Smith and Sidney Rigdon saw those in the Terrestrial or middle Kingdom,

we saw the glory of the terrestrial which excels in all things the glory of the telestial, even in glory, and in power, and in might, and in dominion."[289]

Those in the Terrestrial Kingdom have a higher status but are judged on the same basis, being good people and doing good works. Each person's works will be different. However, the glory of those in the Terrestrial Kingdom is likened unto the moon which suggests that all would have the same glory if they are in the Terrestrial Kingdom. However, the kingdom or responsibility may be different for each individual. This comment is suggested by Joseph when he said each person would have a mansion "*each in his own order.* [290]"

There is one other thing that should be mentioned about those in the Terrestrial Kingdom. It is that the Savior will visit those in the Terrestrial Kingdom,

---

[287] D&C 76;111
[288] D&C 76:112
[289] D&C 76:91
[290] Smith, History of the Church Vol 6, P 365

> *These are they **who receive of the presence of the Son**, but not of the fulness of the Father.* [291]

However, the administration of the Terrestrial will be done by angels appointed to do that function, undoubtedly by directions coming ultimately from the Savior.[292] The Lord said this about kingdoms:

> *All kingdoms have a law given;*
>
> *And there are many kingdoms; for there is no space in the which there is no kingdom; and there is no kingdom in which there is no space, either a greater or a lesser kingdom.*
>
> *And unto every kingdom is given a law; and unto every law there are certain bounds also and conditions.* [293]

Every individual except the sons of perdition will have a dominion, kingdom or mansion of some kind following the final judgment.

SONS OF PERDITION

There is a considerable misunderstanding about who are or can become sons of perdition. Many members have the impression there are only a few people who have become sons of perdition. In actuality there are many more than a few.

Qualifications

Many members have read Joseph Smith's statement about sons of perdition which interpreted means only a few have committed this sin. In actuality he made comments about sons of perdition on Sunday, April 7, 1844 which was recorded by Willard Richards, Wilford Woodruff, Thomas Bullock and Clayton Powell. Willard Richards was a clerk for Joseph at that time and his copy was placed in Joseph Smith's diary,

> *Jesus Christ will save all except the sons of perdition. What must a man do to commit the unpardonable sin? **They must receive the Holy Ghost, have the heavens opened unto them, and know God, and then sin against him.***

---

[291] D&C 76:77
[292] D&C 76:86-88
[293] D&C 88:36-38.

Wilford Woodruff's record of the same talk. This quote is substantiated by the other records made on the same day.

Wilford Woodruff continued,

> *This is the case with many apostates in this church. They never ceased to try to hurt me. They have got the same spirit the devil had. You cannot save them. They make open war like the devil.*[294]

Thomas Bullock recorded this from the same talk regarding apostates,

> *When a man begins to be an enemy, he hunts him (Joseph Smith)* - ***for he has the same spirit that they had who crucified the Lord of life*** - *the same spirit that sends* [sins] *against the Holy Ghost.*[295]

Joseph's diary of the same talk states a person,

> *cannot commit the unpardonable sin after the dissolution of the body.*[296]

These quotes help us to get a more comprehensive understanding of people who commit the sin which makes them sons of perdition. From these quotes we see that:

1. Joseph states that
    a. the heavens must be opened unto them,
    b. know God,
    c. then sin against him.
2. Church apostates have and were committing this sin.
3. Those who crucified the Savior committed this sin.
4. This sin can only be committed in mortality.

In this talk Joseph identified more than just a few who have committed the sin against the Holy Ghost. They include church apostates and those who crucified the Savior.

Consider this question, "How were the heavens opened to those who crucified the Savior?" There is nothing in the Scriptures that clearly shows how the heavens were opened to them. It is easier to

---

[294] Ehat, Words of Joseph Smith, P 347
[295] Ehat, Words of Joseph Smith, P 353
[296] Ehat, Words of Joseph Smith, P 342

understand how the heavens might be opened to apostates but not to those who crucified the Savior.

The Savior revealed this about the sons of perdition:

> *Thus saith the Lord concerning all those who know my power, and have been made partakers thereof, and suffered themselves through the power of the devil to be overcome, and to deny the truth and defy my power –*
>
> *They are they who are the sons of perdition, of whom I say that it had been better for them never to have been born;*
>
> *For they are vessels of wrath, doomed to suffer the wrath of God, with the devil and his angels in eternity;*
>
> **Concerning whom I have said there is no forgiveness in this world nor in the world to come -**[297]

From this quote we learn the following:

1. They must know God's power
2. Have been made partakers thereof
3. They will be returned to Satan's control following their resurrection
4. They have "no forgiveness in this world nor in the world to come"

When the Scriptures have the expression *"no forgiveness in this world or in the world to come"*, it is referring to the sin that makes a man a son of perdition. All others who are not sons of perdition will have a forgiveness given because they will have a salvation of some glory be it small or great.

The Lord said of the sons of perdition,

> *Wherefore, he saves all except them - they shall go away into everlasting punishment, which is endless punishment, which is eternal punishment, to reign with the devil and his angels in eternity,* **where their worm dieth not and the fire is not quenched which is their torment -**[298]

---

[297] D&C 76:31-34
[298] D&C 76:44

When the final judgment is given, the Savior will destroy Satan and his works.[299] Where Satan and his hosts will be placed is not known. It is sometimes referred to as outer darkness. It will not be in the Celestial, Terrestrial or Telestial Kingdoms. The Savior said of Satan's place and punishment,

And the end thereof, neither the place thereof, nor their torment, no man knows;

Neither was it revealed, neither is, neither will be revealed unto man, except to them who are made partakers thereof;

Nevertheless, I, the Lord, show it by vision unto many, but straightway shut it up again;[300]

This book describes three (3) ways to sin and become a son of perdition. The justification for these categories will be identified in the explanation of each category. They are

- Murder – Shedding Innocent Blood
- Holy Ghost – Denying Christ
- Knowing God's Power

Some who are sons of perdition qualify in more than one category.

Murder – Shedding Innocent Blood

Innocent blood is the taking of life without justification. Certainly, the Nephites were not guilty of shedding innocent blood when they fought and killed Lamanites in battle. They were defending themselves, their families and their liberties. The blood they shed was not innocent.

The Lord revealed to Joseph Smith the following:

And now, behold, I speak unto the church. Thou shalt not kill; and ***he that kills shall not have forgiveness in this world, nor in the world to come.***

And again, I say, thou shalt not kill; but he that killeth shall die. [301]

---

[299] D&C 19:3
[300] D&C 76:46–48
[301] D&C 42:18–19

The identification that this verse identifies a son of perdition is the expression that the killer has no "*forgiveness in this world, nor the world to come.*" If a person is a member of the church, they have received the Holy Ghost. If they kill a person and shed innocent blood, they become a son of perdition because they have been blessed with the Holy Ghost. They have committed the unpardonable sin.

Joseph Smith said,

> *The **unpardonable sin** is to shed innocent blood, or **be accessory thereto**.* [302]

Using the expression "unpardonable sin" is the same as saying "*no forgiveness in this world nor in the world to come.*" To commit this sin, one has to "*shed innocent blood, or **become accessory** thereto.*" They do not have to commit the murder themselves.

Probably the most famous example of shedding innocent blood is Judas Iscariot. Judas did not actually commit the murder but took action to help arrest the Savior who was tried, condemned and crucified. When Judas understood the effect of what he had done he realized he had committed the unpardonable sin. He had become a son of perdition for he is quoted as saying,

> *I have sinned in that I have betrayed the innocent blood* [303]

Cain is perhaps the second most famous. Cain killed his brother, Abel. He was taught by angels and had conversed directly with the Lord. In fact, it was the Lord who condemned Cain[304]. Certainly, he qualified as knowing the Lord and he still committed the murder of Abel for gain. Cain loved Satan more than God.[305] Cain was the first to commit murder and Cain is known as "Perdition."[306] It should be remembered that Satan is also known as Perdition.[307] Consequently, those who know God and then follow Satan become Satan's follower or Cain's son or are "Sons of Perdition" because they will suffer the same punishment as Cain.

---

[302] Smith, History of the Church Vol 5, P 392
[303] Matthew 27:4
[304] Genesis 4:9-11
[305] Moses 5:28-33
[306] Moses 5:24
[307] D&C 76:25-27

It appears that Laman and Lemuel became sons of perdition. When Nephi made tools to build a ship which was to take the group to their promised land, the brothers rebelled. Nephi recounted the travels and activities of the Israelites under the leadership of Moses. Then he had this to say about his brothers:

> *Wherefore, the Lord commanded my father that he should depart into the wilderness; and the Jews also sought to take away his life; yea, and* **ye also have sought to take away his** [Lehi's] **life; wherefore, ye are murderers in your hearts** *and ye are like unto them.*
>
> *Ye are swift to do iniquity but slow to remember the Lord your God.* **Ye have seen an angel, and he spake unto you; yea, ye have heard his voice from time to time**; *and he hath spoken unto you in a still small voice, but ye were past feeling, that ye could not feel his words;* **wherefore, he has spoken unto you like unto the voice of thunder, which did cause the earth to shake as if it were to divide asunder.**[308]

The brothers were afraid and helped build the ship. After they arrived at the promised land, they tried to kill Nephi.[309] They thirsted for the blood of Nephi. After Nephi and his group separated themselves from Laman and Lemuel, his brothers waged war against them. Nephi, using the sword of Laban, defended his group but was not killed.[310]

Certainly, Laman and Lemuel had enough experiences to know God. They waged war and were responsible for the shedding of innocent blood of Nephi's group. It is not known whether they directly had killed any of Nephi's followers but they were, as Joseph Smith stated, accessories to or instigators of these killings.

Laman and Lemuel became sons of perdition because they caused innocent blood to be shed and were murderers in their hearts, ignoring having seen an angel and hearing the voice of God.

---

[308] 1 Nephi 17:44-45
[309] 2 Nephi 5:1-3
[310] Jacob 1:10

However, their children were not sons of perdition because they were taught to kill from their parents. In fact, Lehi blessed their children that their parents would be held accountable for their sins. [311]

David's Murder of Uriah

When David became king, he had many wives and concubines that were given to him by temple marriage. The Lord said,

> *David's wives and concubines were given unto him of me, by the hand of Nathan, my servant, and others of the **prophets who had the keys of this power**; and in none of these things did he sin against me save in the case of Uriah and his wife; and, **therefore he hath fallen from his exaltation***[312]

Notice that the prophets who performed the marriages "had keys of this power." These keys were the sealing keys of the priesthood. So, David was married in the new and everlasting covenant.

David and Bathsheba committed adultery and Bathsheba became with child. David personally interviewed Uriah, her husband, and during that conversation tried to get Uriah to go home so that the adultery could be concealed. However, Uriah did not go home.[313]

To avoid Bathsheba being stoned for having committed adultery, David sent a note to Joab, his commander, saying,

> *Set ye Uriah in the forefront of the hottest battle, and retire ye from him, that he may be smitten, and die.*[314]

Uriah died in battle because of David's command.

The Lord had this to say about those who receive the new and everlasting covenant or the marriage covenant and shed innocent blood:

> *The <u>blasphemy against the Holy Ghost</u>, **which shall not be forgiven in the world nor out of the world, is in that ye commit murder wherein ye shed innocent blood**, and assent unto my death, **after ye have received my new and everlasting covenant**,*

---

[311] 2 Nephi 3, 5-6
[312] D&C 132:39
[313] 2 Samuel 11:2-18
[314] 2 Samuel 11:15 (6-17)

saith the Lord God; and he that abideth not this law can in nowise enter into my glory, but shall be damned, saith the Lord.[315]

When Uriah died, David had shed innocent blood by his command to Joab.

The Lord had this to say about the sons of perdition:

Thus saith the Lord concerning all those who know my power, and have been made partakers thereof, and suffered themselves through the power of the devil to be overcome, **and to deny the truth and defy my power—**"[316]

David never did deny Christ nor defy his power but he did commit blasphemy against the Holy Ghost by the murder of Uriah. He lost his exaltation. His wives were given to another.[317] According to the revelation on the sons of perdition he was not to have forgiveness in this world nor in the world to come. Not having this forgiveness means that he would be returned to the torment of Satan after his resurrection and would have no hope of changing that eternally.

David knew of his situation and knew he would suffer in hell throughout eternity. Nevertheless, David tried to repent by sincerely petitioning the Lord for forgiveness. He spent a long time in this repentance process. The Lord did not grant him forgiveness in this world and he is suffering the torment of Satan in hell. However, David received a promise that his soul would not be left in hell. David received this message with gladness for he recorded,

Therefore my heart is glad, and my glory rejoiceth: my flesh also shall rest in hope.

For thou wilt not leave my soul in hell.[318]

Since his soul would not be left in hell, he would receive forgiveness at his resurrection. It is because of David's sincere repentance, not denying Christ nor defying Christ but giving Christ his love and devotion over a period of years that the Lord finally granted that his

---

[315] D&C 132:27

[316] D&C 76:31

[317] D&C 132:38–39

[318] Psalms 16:9–10

soul would not be left in hell. Joseph Smith confirmed this in a sermon on 10 March 1844. According to Franklin D. Richards he said,

> *because that he* [David] *had not spoken against the spirit and because that he had not done this he obtained the promise that God would not leave his soul in hell.*[319]

When a person becomes a son of perdition, his attitude and conduct changes. These changes are described as "**to deny the truth and defy my power**—"[320] Joseph Smith describes this conduct as,

> <u>When a man begins to be an enemy</u> **to this work**, **he hunts me, he seeks to kill me, and never ceases to thirst for my blood. He gets the spirit of the devil-the same spirit that they had who crucified the Lord of Life-the same spirit that sins against the Holy Ghost.**
>
> **You cannot save such persons; you cannot bring them to repentance; they make open war, like the devil, and awful is the consequence.** [321]

After the martyrdom of Joseph and Hyrum Smith on July 27, 1844, three members of the Quorum of the Twelve, W. W. Phelps, Willard Richards and John Taylor wrote a communication dated July 1, 1844, to members of the Church. They counseled the members to not seek retribution for these deaths. They were to be peaceable and calm letting the authorities do their duty. They continued by saying if the authorities did not do their job in prosecuting the murderers it should be left to God. Near the end they penned,

> *and blessed are they that hold out faithful to the end,* **while apostates, consenting to the shedding of innocent blood, have no forgiveness in this world nor in the world to come.**[322]

By this statement they are saying that apostates having the attitude of wanting to kill Church leaders or "consenting" thereto would be sons of perdition. This seems to suggest that members who apostatize and then want to kill or do harm to the Church leaders become sons of

---

[319] Ehat, Words of Joseph Smith P 335

[320] D&C 76:31

[321] Smith, History of the Church Vol 6, P 315

[322] Smith, History of the Church Vol 7, P 152

perdition and have no forgiveness whether they act on that attitude or not.

Holy Ghost – Denying Christ

This section gives more information on those sons of perdition who qualify under this scripture:

> **Having denied the Holy Spirit after having received it, and having denied the Only Begotten Son** of the Father, having crucified him unto themselves and put him to an open shame.[323]

Joseph Smith had this to say:

> *All sins shall be forgiven, except the sin against the Holy Ghost; for Jesus will save all except the sons of perdition. What must a man do to commit the unpardonable sin? He must receive the Holy Ghost, have the heavens opened unto him, and know God, and then sin against him. After a man has sinned against the Holy Ghost, there is no repentance for him. He has got to say that the sun does not shine while he sees it; he has got to deny Jesus Christ when the heavens have been opened unto him, and to deny the plan of salvation with his eyes open to the truth of it; and from that time he begins to be an enemy.* [324]

Some members of the Church have read this quote and claim that this is the only way to become a son of perdition because Joseph Smith said this quote. This view is totally misplaced as we have shown that they can become a son of perdition by shedding innocent blood. However, this quote describes this category well. Note that Joseph stated that these sons of perdition fight against God as Satan does now.

Sherem

Jacob, the younger brother of Nephi, experienced an encounter with one Sherem who was preaching that there was no Christ and that Jacob was teaching false doctrines.[325] Jacob confounded Sherem following which Sherem asked for a sign. Jacob declined to give a sign but said that if it were the will of God that a sign would be

---

[323] D&C 76:31-35, See also Alma 39:5-6
[324] Smith, History of the Church vol 6, P 314
[325] Jacob 7:6-7

given. Sherem was overcome and fell to the earth. He was nourished for several days. Sherem then asked that the people to be brought together so that he could speak to them,

> And he spake plainly unto them, that he had been deceived by the power of the devil. And he spake of hell, and of eternity, and of eternal punishment.
>
> And he said: **I fear lest I have committed the <u>unpardonable sin</u>**, for I have lied unto God; for I denied the Christ, and said that I believed the scriptures; and they truly testify of him. And because I have thus lied unto God I greatly fear lest my case shall be awful; but I confess unto God
>
> And it came to pass that when he had said these words he could say no more, and he gave up the ghost. [326]

Korihor

Korihor was a person who went from land to land within the Nephite territory preaching against the church by telling people that there was no God. He taught that the Nephites were in bondage to the performances and ordinances laid down by ancient priests. He also said that looking forward to a "remission of your sins" was the result of a "frenzied mind" and that "this derangement of your minds" [327] was because of traditions. He said that they believed in things that were not so.

Eventually he was confronted by Alma which resulted in Korihor pressing for a sign. Finally, Alma gave him a sign and Korihor was struck dumb. Following this curse Korihor wrote,

> I know that I am dumb, for I cannot speak; and I know that nothing save it were the power of God could bring this upon me; yea, and **I always knew that there was a God.**
>
> But behold, the devil hath deceived me; for he appeared unto me in the form of an angel, and said unto me: Go and reclaim this people, for they have all gone astray after an unknown God. And he said unto me: There is no God; yea, and he taught me that which I should say. And I have taught his words; and I taught

---

[326] Jacob 7:18-20
[327] Alma 30:12-16

them because they were pleasing unto the carnal mind; and I taught them, even until I had much success, insomuch that I verily believed that they were true; and for this cause I withstood the truth, even until I have brought this great curse upon me. [328]

Nehor

Another example is Nehor. Nehor set up a separate church and contended against the church of God. He taught that all would be saved and would have eternal life no matter what they did. He taught that the priests and teachers should be "popular" and supported by the people.[329] He contended against Gideon who was instrumental in planning and getting King Limhi's people away from Lamanite bondage. When Nehor could not best Gideon he drew his sword and killed Gideon.

He was bound and brought before Alma to be judged according to the crimes that he committed. Nehor had practiced "priest craft" and tried to enforce it with the sword. Nehor had shed the innocent blood of righteous Gideon. He was condemned to die for his crimes and just before his death, he acknowledged *"that what he had taught to the people was contrary to the word of God."* [330] Nehor knew what the truth was and denied that knowledge by teaching against it. In doing so he became a son of perdition prior to killing Gideon. By killing Gideon, he shed innocent blood, which also qualified him to become a son of perdition.

However, Nehor had set up churches and followers who continued his teachings. Some of these groups migrated to live among the Lamanites and encouraged the Lamanites to fight against the Nephites from time to time. It is probable that these groups became sons of perditions when they continued the fight against the Nephites or killed Lamanite converts.

Lamanite Converts

Ammon and his brethren undertook a mission to the Lamanites and converted a large number of Lamanites. After a time, other Lamanites became angry with them and made war to destroy them. The converts

---

[328] Alma 30:52–53
[329] Alma 1:3-4
[330] Alma 1:7-15

did not resist and a thousand were slain. The warring Lamanites stopped fighting and many of this warring group were converted and joined the converts. Mormon describes this warring group as,

> Now the greatest number of those of the Lamanites who slew so many of their brethren were Amalekites and Amulonites, **the greatest number of whom were after the order of the Nehors.**
>
> Now, among those who joined the people of the Lord there were not one who were Amalekites or Amulonites, or who were after the order of the Nehor, but they were actual descendants of Laman and Lemuel.[331]

The Amalekites and Amulonites were Nephites who dissented from them and lived among the Lamanites. They are the ones who did most of the killing in this massacre, so these dissenters actually murdered the Savior's people and shed innocent blood as the converted Lamanites did not defend themselves. Then Mormon makes this observation about these Amalekites and Amulonites,

> And thus we can plainly discern, that after a people have been once enlightened by the Spirit of God, and have had great knowledge of things pertaining to righteousness, and then have fallen away into sin and transgression, they become more hardened, and thus their state becomes worse than those who had never known these things.[332]

These Amalekites and Amulonites were shedding innocent blood. Since their roots were among the Nephites, they were taught differently and converted to become Nehors, who were against God. They settled among the Lamanites and influenced them against the Lamanite converts. Their killing of the Lamanite converts and shedding their innocent blood was furthering their fight against God. They were sons of perdition.

Knowing God's Power

The Lord chastised the people in the cities of Chorazin, Bethsaida and Capernaum by saying,

---

[331] Alma 24:28-29
[332] Alma 24:30

> *Then began he to upbraid the cities **wherein most of his mighty works were done, because they repented not:***
>
> *Woe unto thee, Chorazin! woe unto thee, Bethsaida! for if the mighty works, which were done in you, had been done in Tyre and Sidon, they would have repented long ago in sackcloth and ashes.*
>
> *But I say unto you, **It shall be more tolerable for Tyre and Sidon at the day of judgment, than for you.***
>
> *And thou, **Capernaum, which art exalted unto heaven, shalt be brought down to hell**: for if the mighty works, which have been done in thee, had been done in Sodom, it would have remained until this day.*
>
> *But I say unto you, That **it shall be <u>more tolerable</u> for the land of Sodom in the day of judgment, than for thee.***[333]

When the Lord named these cities, he was speaking of the people living within those cities. We should recognize that some individuals within these groups were good people. The Savior called Peter, James and John to follow him while they were in Capernaum. There probably were some people in the cities that had been healed and otherwise blessed that may have accepted Christ as their Savior and repented. However, these were few in comparison to the group as a whole.

Although the Savior compared Chorazin and Bethsaida to Tyre and Sidon and then compared Capernaum to Sodom he gave the same judgment statement to each of them.

On the one hand there are the wicked cities of Tyre, Sidon, and Sodom. Sodom and Gomorrah with several other cities were destroyed by fire from heaven.[334] They were destroyed to make an example of them because of their wickedness.[335] The people of those cities were in hell at the time of the Savior. They are in hell at the present time awaiting their resurrection and the final judgment

---

[333] Matthew 11:20–25
[334] Genesis 19:23-28
[335] 2 Peter 2:6, Jude 1:7

following which they will generally be consigned to the Telestial Kingdom. Their fate at the time of the Savior was already known.

On the other hand, the cities of Chorazin, Bethsaida and Capernaum, in which *"most of his mighty works were done",* were still living at the time the Savior made his statement. By the Savior's statement the people in those cities had not repented and were still wicked in spite of seeing these mighty miracles. They should have known that he was the son of God by these miracles.

The Savior said that it would be *"more tolerable"* or acceptable for those people of Tyre, Sidon, and Sodom at the *"day of judgment"* than for the people of Chorazin, Bethsaida and Capernaum.

The day of judgment is referring to the final judgment at the end of the world, which is where eternal habitations are finalized. By this statement the Lord means that at the day of judgment, the people of Tyre, Sidon, and Sodom will have a better judgment outcome than the people of Chorazin, Bethsaida, and Capernaum.

The wicked people in the cities of Tyre, Sidon and Sodom will generally be consigned to the Telestial Kingdom. If the people in Chorazin, Bethsaida and Capernaum were consigned to the Telestial Kingdom, there would be no difference in their final judgment and the Savior's statement would be meaningless.

The only judgment that would be different and less tolerable (or more severe) is for those in the cities of Chorazin, Bethsaida and Capernaum to be consigned to be with Satan through all eternity. and consequently, they would be sons of perdition having no forgiveness in the world to come.

The question is, "What is the gospel standard that would make the people of Chorazin, Bethsaida and Capernaum be sons of perdition?" The pertinent scripture is:

> *Thus saith the Lord concerning all **those who know my power, and have been made partakers thereof, and suffered themselves through the power of the devil to be overcome, and to deny the truth and defy my power.***

> *They are they who are the sons of perdition, of whom I say that it had been better for them never to have been born.*[336]

How does one know of God's power and be made partakers thereof? They know and are made partakers of his power by the miracles performed. Well did Nicodemus state the principle of how the people should respond to the Savior performing "mighty miracles" when he addressed the Savior:

> *Rabbi, we know that thou art a teacher come from God: **for no man can do these miracles that thou doest, except God be with him.***[337]

Having mighty miracles performed among them is the same as knowing God's power because they witnessed these miracles. Jacob, Nephi's brother, quoted an angel as saying that the Savior:

> *should come among the Jews, among those who are the more wicked part of the world; and they shall crucify him—for thus it behooveth our God, and there is none other nation on earth that would crucify their God.*
>
> ***For should the mighty miracles be wrought among other nations <u>they would repent, and know that he be their God</u>.***[338]

The Savior spoke of John the Baptist and his testimony or light concerning the Savior and said,

> *But I have greater witness than that of John: **for the works which the Father hath given me to finish, the same works that I do, <u>bear witness of me</u>,** that the Father hath sent me.*[339]

His works include the miracles he performed! Having seen the Savior's miracles or power classify the inhabitants as knowing his power and turning from him to crucify him makes them sons of perdition.

---

[336] D&C 76:31-32
[337] John 3:2
[338] 2 Nephi 10:3-4
[339] John 5:36

The soldiers who were cruel to the Savior are not Sons of Perdition. When the Savior was on the cross, he asked the Father to forgive the soldiers. Luke wrote,

> *Then said Jesus, Father, **forgive them**; for they know not what they do [meaning the soldiers who maltreated and crucified him]. And they parted his raiment, and cast lots.*[340]

The Savior was totally silent with regard to the Jewish leaders and others who demanded his death. The Jewish leaders knew of Christ's miracles. They saw many healed and many other miracles were reported to them. The same thing can be said of these Jewish leaders as was written regarding the people of Chorazin, Bethsaida and Capernaum.

The Jewish leadership should have known, as Nicodemus did, that he was the Messiah. Instead, they were seeking to kill him. They had previously decided to arrange killing him because his miracles and actions interrupted their income and authority.[341]

However, the Jewish leadership feared the people and did not know how they would react.[342] Therefore, with the help of Judas Iscariot, the Jewish leaders arrested the Savior at night and began their judgments out of the sight and knowledge of the people. The Jewish leaders and those who cried for the crucifixion of Christ became sons of perdition by their key role in murdering Christ.

Joseph Smith said,

> *When a man begins to be an enemy to this work, he hunts me, he seeks to kill me, and never ceases to thirst for my blood. He **gets the spirit of the devil-the same spirit that they had who crucified the Lord of Life-the <u>same spirit that sins against the Holy Ghost.</u>***[343]

We can see from these scriptures of the extreme wickedness of the people of Chorazin, Bethsaida and Capernaum and the Jewish

---

[340] Luke 23:34 with footnote, see JST Luke 23:35
[341] Matthew 26:3-4
[342] Mark 11:18, Mark 12:12, Luke 20:19, Luke 22:2
[343] Smith, History of the Church Vol 6, P 315

leadership. This wickedness had extreme consequences for the nation. Quoting the prophet Zenos, Nephi wrote,

> And as for those who are at Jerusalem, saith the prophet, they shall be scourged by all people, because **they crucify the God of Israel, and turn their hearts aside, <u>rejecting signs and wonders</u>, and the power and glory of the God of Israel**.
>
> And because they turn their hearts aside, saith the prophet, and have despised the Holy One of Israel, they shall wander in the flesh, and perish, and become a hiss and a byword, and be hated among all nations.
>
> Nevertheless, when that day cometh, saith the prophet, that they no more turn aside their hearts against the Holy One of Israel, then will he remember the covenants which he made to their fathers. [344]

We need to be careful and not ascribe the request of the Savior to forgive the soldiers for his crucifixion as requesting the forgiveness of those who are sons of perdition and caused his death. As did the Savior, we should remain silent as their acts condemned them as sons of perdition.

THE MILLENNIUM

This is not a comprehensive review of this subject. Others have written extensively of this subject.

This is a period of resurrection, growth, development and preparation for the final events of the earth. The Savior will dwell on the earth through this entire period. The major event following this period is the final judgment at which every person will receive their eternal consignment.

Consuming Fire

God and the Savior, who is in God's presence, has been described as living in flaming flames and that mortals will be consumed in his presence. One such quote reads,

---

[344] 1 Nephi 19:13-16

> *God dwells in flaming flames and he is a consuming fire he will consume all that is unclean and unholy*[345]

The Savior stated the following about his coming to be on the earth during the millennium,

> *the day of my coming in a pillar of fire,*[346]

He will come to the earth bringing his flaming flames which will cover the earth. This is an important concept because it relates to how the proud and wicked will be destroyed at the beginning of the millennium. There are three scriptures in the Doctrine & Covenants that state the Savior will "*burn them up*" referring to the wicked. One of those scriptures reads,

> *For the hour is nigh and the day soon at hand when the earth is ripe; and <u>all the proud and they that do wickedly</u> shall be as stubble; and I **will burn them** up, saith the Lord of Hosts, **that wickedness shall not be upon the earth** ...*

> *For I will reveal myself from heaven with power and great glory, with all the hosts thereof, and **dwell in righteousness with men on earth a thousand years**, and the wicked shall not stand.*[347]

The Savior states that he will "*burn them up*" so that "*wickedness shall not be upon the earth.*"

It is because he dwells in flaming fire that will cover the earth at his coming. This fire will burn up the proud and the wicked. This will happen as the Savior comes to the earth at the beginning of the millennium. In addition, Satan will have no power over the surviving mortal people and will not be able to tempt them.[348]

With no wickedness on the earth and Satan having no ability to tempt people, the earth will be in a Terrestrial state.

Mortality

The Lord has this to say about the parable of the ten virgins,

---

[345] The Words of Joseph Smith, P 371
[346] D&C 29:12
[347] D&C 29:9, 11
[348] D&C 45:55

And at that day, when I shall come in my glory, shall the parable be fulfilled which I spake concerning the ten virgins.

*For **they that are wise and have received the truth, and have taken the Holy Spirit for their guide, and have not been deceived**—verily I say unto you, <u>they shall not be hewn down and cast into the fire, but shall abide the day</u>.*

*And the earth shall be given unto them for an inheritance; and they shall multiply and wax strong, **and their children shall grow up without sin unto salvation.***

*For **the Lord shall be in their midst, and his glory shall be upon them, and he will be their king and their lawgiver.**[349]*

It appears from the language of this quote that the unwise virgins *"shall be hew down and cast into the fire."* That fire is the consuming fire that will cleanse the earth at the Savior's coming.

The reason that the wise virgins can be in the presence of the Savior is that they *"have received the truth, and have taken the Holy Spirit for their guide."* The Holy Ghost makes it possible that they can be in the Savior's presence. There were promises made in this quote to those who qualify. It is *"their children shall grow up without sin unto salvation."* This will happen because the parents will teach them righteous principles. Satan will not be there to tempt them.

There have been statements made by apostles especially by Brigham Young, that men (and women) of other faiths would be living during the millennium. These would be people who have a *"testimony of the Savior"* and have conducted their lives in accordance with that testimony. They would be able to have children. They would be responsible to raise them and probably teach them to have a *"testimony of the Savior."*

And when they die, they will become immortal in the "twinkling of an eye."

All Resurrections
The first resurrection event was recorded in the New Testament,

---

[349] D&C 45:56-59

> *And the graves were opened; and many bodies of the saints which slept arose,*
>
> *And came out of the graves after his resurrection, and went into the holy city, and appeared unto many.*[350]

Those who were resurrected at this time were the righteous people, worthy of eternal life. They had died from the time of Adam until the time of the Savior. The wicked people from this period are still in hell suffering from Satan. No one has been resurrected since this resurrection event.

The next resurrection event will occur when the Savior descends to the earth at the beginning of the millennium. As he descends to the earth,

> *an angel shall sound his trump, and the saints that have slept shall come forth to meet me in the cloud.*[351]

The Savior further describes this resurrection,

> *For a trump shall sound both long and loud, even as upon Mount Sinai, and all the earth shall quake, and they shall come forth— yea, even the dead which died in me, to receive a crown of righteousness, and to be clothed upon, even as I am, to be with me, that we may be one.*[352]

This resurrection will include all of those worthy adults who have died from the first resurrection until this resurrection. They will have made righteous choices and be worthy to return to his presence. This would include all and only those, who are worthy of eternal life for this resurrection. Speaking further of this resurrection, the Savior said,

> *Wherefore, if ye have slept in peace blessed are you; for as you now behold me and know that I am, even so shall ye come unto me and **your souls shall live, and your redemption shall be perfected**; and the saints shall come forth from the four quarters of the earth.*[353]

---

[350] Matthew 27:52-53
[351] D&C 45:45
[352] D&C 29:13
[353] D&C 45:46

The possibility of our seeing the Savior during our mortality is very unlikely. There are some who have seen the Savior during their mortal period but they are few in comparison to the total population of the Church. When we live righteously and then die, we will likely *"sleep in peace."* When we are resurrected to meet him, we will behold him and know who he is. Our souls shall live and our *"redemption shall be perfected."* This statement suggests that there must be more to learn before we enter the presence of the Father. This discussion describes those who are worthy to be with the Savior at his coming.

However, during the millennium there will be multiple groups who will be resurrected,

> *And then shall the heathen nations be redeemed, and they that knew no law shall have part in the first resurrection; and it shall be tolerable for them.*[354]

The expression "first resurrection" identifies the resurrections that will occur during this millennium. There will be many resurrections that will occur during this period. All people from around the world worthy of being part of the first resurrection will be resurrected during this period. The heathen nations are examples of this principle. This will be a part of the preparation for the final judgment, which is when we will receive our eternal consignment.

The only group that will not be resurrected during this period will be those in hell suffering under Satan. The Lord stated this about those who inherit the Telestial Kingdom,

> *These are they who are thrust down to hell.*
>
> *These are they who shall not be redeemed from the devil until the last resurrection, until the Lord, even Christ the Lamb, shall have finished his work.*[355]

Mortals will be resurrected when they are changed *"in the twinkling of an eye."*

Resurrected Babies

---

[354] D&C 45:54
[355] D&C 76:84-85

No babies or children who died before the age of accountability will be resurrected at the coming of the Savior. Only adult "saints" will be resurrected to join the Savior in the "cloud", which means they will be righteous adults. Since babies and little children are sinless and pure, they are entitled to the full blessings of the Father.

In the section "Little Children" it was shown that Agnes Smith, wife of Don Carlos Smith, will raise and teach her daughter following her resurrection. Her daughter's name is Sophronia. In order for Sophronia to be in the Celestial Kingdom, she will have to be raised and taught by her mother until she has grown to maturity. Then she will,

- Have a mortal sister perform her temple ordinances
- Identify a male companion to marry
- Have the proxy marriage performed in the temple
- Eventually be admitted into Father's presence as entitled to eternal life.

This model will be required for every baby or young child who has died because they are sinless and pure. If a parent is not available because of unrighteousness, then a grandparent, aunt or other relative would be chosen to raise the child to maturity. But every baby or young child will need a "parent" to teach them what they need to learn. When they have been sufficiently taught, they will make the decisions for ordinances to be performed to accomplish their eternal life.

One last thought:

Can you imagine a newborn baby who died, being resurrected in the same form? There would have to be a "parent" immediately available to hold and cuddle that baby. That resurrected baby would have the same needs as a mortal baby.

Final Judgment

At the end of the millennium the earth will be spared for a short time,

> *And again, verily, verily, I say unto you that when the thousand years are ended, and men again begin to deny their God, then will I spare the earth but for a little season;*[356]

There are several things that need to be accomplished before the very end of the earth in its present form. One of those things is to complete the resurrection of all who have not been resurrected,

> *But, behold, verily I say unto you, before the earth shall pass away, Michael, mine archangel, shall sound his trump, and **then shall all the dead awake, for their graves shall be opened, and they shall come forth—yea, even all.***[357]

The expression *"yea, even all"* identifies that the remaining souls who have not been resurrected, will be resurrected at this time. This final group are those who are in hell, sufferings from Satan. But Satan and his spirit followers are not resurrected. They remain in spirit form forever.

So, after this resurrection, all humankind will be alive upon the earth in their resurrected state. These will include sons of perdition, Telestial Kingdom people, Terrestrial Kingdom people and those that will be in the Celestial Kingdom. Also, on the earth will be Satan and his spirit followers, who were placed here prior to Adam and Eve.

But all of these beings cannot stay on the earth. Only those who will be in the Celestial Kingdom, can be on the earth. Those who are worthy of eternal life will gather their "posterity" about them ready to inhabit the earth, when it is glorified.

Satan with his followers and Sons of Perdition will need to be placed in outer darkness by the Savior and those that may assist him. The Telestial Kingdom people will need to be transported to a planet on which they will reside throughout eternity. The word planet is used because all Telestial people will be resurrected and will have physical bodies. They will not be floating throughout the universe and they will not be on the earth after it is changed. The same will happen to the Terrestrial Kingdom people. They will also need a physical place to reside.

---

[356] D&C 29:22
[357] D&C 29:26

If we survey what we know about the universe, we can only conclude that a planet of sufficient size is the only object that would accommodate these resurrected people. Those left on the earth following this physical placement, will be residents in the Celestial Kingdom.

The earth will be changed to be the Celestial Kingdom,

> *And the end shall come, and the heaven and the earth shall be consumed and pass away, and there shall be a new heaven and a new earth.*
>
> ***And the righteous shall be gathered on my right hand unto eternal life;*** [358]
>
> *And the end shall come, and the heaven and the earth shall be consumed and pass away, and there shall be a new heaven and a new earth.*
>
> *For all old things shall pass away, and **all things shall become new, even the heaven and the earth**, and all the fulness thereof, both men and beasts, the fowls of the air, and the fishes of the sea;*
>
> *And not one hair, neither mote, shall be lost, for it is the workmanship of mine hand.* [359]

Notice that the Celestial Kingdom will have animals, fowls of the air and fish. Also, not one hair of any human or animal will be lost. Every particle relating to the earth will be in its proper place. This is how meticulous and precise the Savior will be when these events will happen.

---

[358] D&C 29:22-23
[359] D&C 29:23-25

■ OTHER SUBJECTS of INTEREST ■

Included here are discussions that do not appear to fit well in the structure of this book. It includes the following

>Law of Moses

>Peter Denying Christ

>Determining Passover Events

Law of Moses

This topic discusses issues about the dealings of Jehovah with the Israelites and his attempts to make them qualified to return to the presence of the Father. As a people they were a chosen people resulting from the righteousness of Abraham, Isaac and Jacob. The implementation of the Law of Moses restricted the general population from receiving the full blessings available from temple ordinances and further restrictions occurred later at the time of Elijah. It includes a few issues not well known or commonly discussed.

Peter Denying Christ

This has been a significant puzzlement to Christians because of Peter's firm testimony of Jesus being the Messiah. This discussion carefully reviews Peter's mindset through the time that he denied the Savior and why the Savior forgave him.

Determining Passover Events

Using the consistency of the Solar system and current knowledge of sunrise and sunset times, projections were made as to the time the Sabbath began and events during the Savior's Passover wherein, he had his meal with apostles, offered his prayers, suffered in the Garden, was arrested and experienced the rest of the events of that night.

LAW OF MOSES

After Moses was exiled from Egypt, he was called to be a prophet. Remember the burning bush experience.[360] Prior to this Moses received the Melchizedek Priesthood from his father-in-law,

---

[360] Exodus 3:1-15

Jethro.[361] The children of Israel were eventually led out of Egypt and traveled through the Sinai Peninsula until they arrived at Mount Sinai. By this time Moses had held the Melchizedek Priesthood for many years. He ordained others to that priesthood as he led the children of Israel out of Egypt and taught them. At Mount Sinai, the Lord gave a number of commandments to Moses who in turn taught them to the Israelites. It is easy to think that Moses only went up to the Mount one time especially after seeing the movie "The Ten Commandments." However, Moses went up a number of times to receive commandments and returned to teach them to the Israelites. He received their commitment to live those teachings. These visits include:

> *The Lord covenants to make Israel a peculiar treasure, a kingdom of priests, and a holy nation—The people sanctify themselves—The Lord appears* (to the people) *on Sinai amid fire, smoke, and earthquakes.*[362]

> *The Lord reveals the Ten Commandments—Israel is to bear witness that the Lord has spoken from heaven—The children of Israel are forbidden to make gods of silver or gold—They are to make altars of unhewn stones and sacrifice to the Lord thereon.*[363]

> *The Lord reveals His laws pertaining to servants, marriage, the death penalty for various offenses, the giving of an eye for an eye and a tooth for a tooth, and the damage done by oxen.*[364]

> *The Lord reveals His laws pertaining to stealing, destructions by fire, care of the property of others, borrowing, lascivious acts, sacrifices to false gods, afflicting widows, usury, reviling God, and the firstborn of men and of animals—The men of Israel are commanded to be holy.*[365]

---

[361] D&C 84:6
[362] Exodus Ch. 19 Heading
[363] Exodus Ch. 20 Heading
[364] Exodus Ch 21 Heading
[365] Exodus Ch 22, Heading

> *The Lord reveals His laws pertaining to integrity and godly conduct—The land is to rest during a sabbatical year—The children of Israel are to keep three annual feasts—An angel, bearing the Lord's name, will guide them—Sickness will be removed—The nations of Canaan will be driven out gradually. "* [366]

> *Israel accepts the word of the Lord by covenant—Moses sprinkles the blood of the covenant—He, Aaron, Nadab, Abihu, and seventy of the elders of Israel see God—The Lord calls Moses on to the mount to receive the tables of stone and commandments.* [367]

These headnote quotes demonstrate that Moses went up many times to talk with the Lord and received instructions which were relayed to Israel.

In the last headnote Moses, Aaron, Nadab, Abihu and seventy of the elders of Israel went up to Mount Sinai and all saw the God of Israel.[368] All of these men who beheld God with Moses held the Melchizedek Priesthood. While Moses led Israel, the Melchizedek Priesthood was active and held by many among the Israelites.

Finally, Moses instructed the people on an important covenant.

> *And he took the **book of the covenant, and read in the audience of the people**: and they said, All that the LORD hath said will we do, and be obedient.*[369]

This "covenant" provided the qualifications for individuals to receive the marriage covenant which Israel accepted and promised obedience.

Moses went back to the mount to receive further instructions from the Lord. These instructions described the Tabernacle of the Congregation. The purpose of this tabernacle was:

> *And let them make me a sanctuary; that I may dwell among them.*[370]

---

[366] Exodus 23, Heading

[367] Exodus 24, Heading

[368] Exodus 24:9-10

[369] Exodus 24:7

[370] Exodus 25:8-9

This was a command to build a sanctuary in which the Lord would dwell! Priesthood keys would be exercised to provide the initiatory, endowment and the marriage covenants. Moses was on the mount for forty days and nights. While he was there the people demonstrated that as a people, they could not live the laws given by Moses from the Book of Covenant. They had built a golden calf, worshiped it and engaged in riotous activities.[371] In the revelation on priesthood to Joseph Smith the Lord said

> *Therefore, in the ordinances thereof* [Melchizedek Priesthood temple ordinances], *the power of godliness is manifest.*
>
> *And without the ordinances thereof, and the authority of the priesthood, the power of godliness is not manifest unto men in the flesh;*
>
> *For without this no man can see the face of God, even the Father, and live. Now this* **Moses plainly taught to the children of Israel in the wilderness***, and sought diligently to sanctify his people that they might behold the face of God;*
>
> *But* **they hardened their hearts** *and could not endure his presence;*
>
> *Therefore,* **he took Moses out of their midst, and the Holy Priesthood also***.*[372]

Because of the worship of the golden calf and the riotous activities the Lord "*took Moses out of their midst, and the Holy Priesthood also.*"[373]

The Holy or Melchizedek Priesthood was taken from "their midst" means that the general population of men in Israel were not eligible to be ordained to that priesthood. Consequently, they could not receive the full temple ordinances that are now available to us. These were replaced by performances and ordinances to point to and have faith in the Savior. These changes included rules of conduct and punishments which became known as the Law of Moses.

---

[371] Exodus 32
[372] D&C 84:20-25
[373] D&C 84:25

The Lord also took Moses "out of their midst." Previously Moses was directly involved in the administration of the people. That stopped. Moses was still the prophet but his relationship to the people changed. Moses continued in the overall leadership of Israel but in a different way.

Moses was instructed to call Aaron and his sons to be priests to administer new performances and ordinances. It is important to note that Nadab and Abihu were sons of Aaron.[374] Moses, Aaron, Nadab and Abihu were all Levites or of the tribe of Levi.[375] They also held the Melchizedek Priesthood.

> *AND take thou unto thee **Aaron thy brother, and his sons with him**, from among the children of Israel, **that he may minister unto me in the priest's office.***[376]
>
> *Bring the tribe of Levi near, and present them <u>before Aaron the priest</u>, that they may minister unto him.*
>
> *And **they shall keep his charge**.*[377]

Aaron had charge of the Levites in the administration of their priest duties and he ministered *"in the priest's office."* Aaron and definitely those that followed would be called the "high priest" which is not to be confused with the office of high priest in the Melchizedek Priesthood. Although Aaron held the Melchizedek Priesthood he functioned as a leader of the priests and administrator over all the activities and duties of the Levitical or Aaronic Priesthood. Thus, he was the "high" priest. When we read of the High Priest or Chief Priest in the New Testament that priest was functioning in a similar capacity as Aaron.

Some of these performances and ordinances were performed in the Tabernacle of the Congregation. The men of the Levite tribe were called as a group and given authority to administer certain ordinances in the Tabernacle of the Congregation and to care for the instruments therein.[378] Zacharias was attending to some of these duties in the

---

[374] Exodus 6:23
[375] 1 Chronicles 23:14
[376] Exodus 28:1
[377] Numbers 3:6-7
[378] Numbers 3:5-9

temple when he was informed by Elias that his wife would give birth to a son.[379] The authority or priesthood was called both the Aaronic Priesthood because Aaron was the first administrator and sometimes called the Levitical Priesthood because the tribe of Levi was called as a group to minister in the Law of Moses. It is the same priesthood.

The Melchizedek Priesthood continued to preside in Israel. Aaron still reported to Moses. Joshua was ordained by Moses to lead Israel following Moses' administration.[380] It is important to note that Joshua did not participate in the worship of the golden calf. He waited for Moses part way up the mountain until Moses came down.[381] Joshua not being a participant in the worship of the calf was worthy to follow Moses as the leader of Israel with the keys of the Melchizedek Priesthood. Joshua directed Israel in many activities including the destruction of the walls of Jericho and the settlement of Israel in that promised land.

The keys within that Priesthood to perform the sacred ordinance of temple marriage were held and administered by following prophets. They performed these sacred ordinances for some worthy people in Israel until Elijah was taken from the earth. For example, King David was married to his wives by the prophet Nathan and others who had the temple sealing keys.[382] David was married to his wives in the Tabernacle of the Congregation. The Tabernacle of the Congregation was used for these sacred ordinances until it was replaced by Solomon's temple. These ordinances pertaining to the marriage covenant were conducted concurrently with those duties of the Aaronic Priesthood in the tabernacle and later in Solomon's temple.

Elijah and the Temple Keys

Elijah lived during the reign of King Ahab of the Northern kingdom of Israel which was about the ninth century prior to the birth of the Savior. In a treatise on the Priesthood Joseph Smith wrote,

> ***Elijah was the last Prophet that held the keys of the Priesthood**, and who will, before the last dispensation, restore the authority*

---

[379] Luke 1:5-14
[380] Deuteronomy 34:8-9
[381] Exodus 32:17-18
[382] D&C 132:39

> *and deliver the keys of the Priesthood, in order that all the ordinances may be attended to in righteousness...'And I will send Elijah the Prophet before the great and terrible day of the Lord'.* **Why send Elijah? Because he holds the keys of the authority to administer in all the ordinances of the Priesthood;** *and without the authority is given, the ordinances could not be administered in righteousness.*[383]

Following Elijah, no living prophet in Israel held the priesthood keys. The taking of the keys of the priesthood from Israel was a very significant event. It affected the priesthood administration process and eliminated the ability for anyone living to receive the marriage covenant sealed by the priesthood keys. Joseph Smith in the marriage covenant revelation revealed that only one person on the earth holds those keys at any one time.

> *All covenants, contracts, bonds, obligations, oaths, vows, performances, connections, associations, or expectations, that are not made and entered into and sealed by the Holy Spirit of promise,* **of him who is anointed**, *both as well for time and for all eternity, and that too most holy, by revelation and commandment through the medium of* **mine anointed, whom I have appointed on the earth to hold this power** *(and I have appointed unto my servant Joseph to hold this power in the last days,* **and there is never but one on the earth at a time on whom this power and the keys of this priesthood are conferred**), *are of no efficacy, virtue, or force in and after the resurrection from the dead; for all contracts that are not made unto this end have an end when men are dead.* [384]"

The important point of this quote for this discussion is that only one person holds these keys of the priesthood at any one point in time on the earth. The President of the Church of Jesus Christ of Latter-day Saints currently holds the active keys in the priesthood. We commonly know that the members of the Quorum of the Twelve and the members of the First Presidency have all been ordained with those keys but only the President is authorized to exercise those keys.

---

[383] Smith, History of the Church Vol 4, P 211
[384] D&C 132:7

In Elijah's time there was no such arrangement. Joseph Smith wrote that Elijah was the last prophet to hold those keys. The events that happened in Elijah's time are very significant to understanding why Elijah took the priesthood keys with him.

King Ahab and Jezebel were very wicked people. They actually worshiped the false god Baal, Jezebel actually killed the existing prophets of the Lord except for one hundred who were saved by a righteous Obadiah[385],

Elijah met with King Ahab and arranged a test between the prophets of Baal and Elijah the prophet of the God of Abraham, Isaac and Jacob.

> *And Elijah came unto all the people, and said, How long halt ye between two opinions? if the LORD be God, follow him: but if Baal, then follow him. And the people answered him not a word.*
>
> *Then said **Elijah unto the people, I, even I only, remain a prophet of the LORD; but Baal's prophets are four hundred and fifty men.***
>
> *Let them therefore give us two bullocks; and let them choose one bullock for themselves, and cut it in pieces, and lay it on wood, and put no fire under: and I will dress the other bullock, and lay it on wood, and put no fire under:*
>
> *And call ye on the name of your gods, and I will call on the name of the LORD: and the God that answereth by fire, let him be God. And all the people answered and said, It is well spoken.*
>
> *And Elijah said unto the prophets of Baal, Choose you one bullock for yourselves, and dress it first; for ye are many; and call on the name of your gods, but put no fire under.*[386]

The test was to see which God would send down fire to consume the offerings.

Elijah stated that he was the only remaining *"prophet of the Lord."* He was the only one who held the priesthood keys. No other prophet that Obadiah may have saved held these same keys and authority.

---

[385] 1 Kings 18:13

[386] 1 Kings 18:21–25

The prophets of Baal failed in their attempt but Elijah's God caused fire to come down and consume Elijah's offering.

Jezebel then sought to kill Elijah and he fled to preserve his life. Elijah then had a conversation with the Lord in which he told the Lord

> *the children of Israel have forsaken thy covenant, thrown down thine altars, and slain thy prophets with the sword; and I, even I only, am left; and they seek my life, to take it away.*[387]

The Lord gave Elijah instructions including the following

> *Elisha the son of Shaphat of Abel-meholah shalt thou anoint to be prophet in thy room.*[388]

Since Elijah was the last prophet to hold these keys, then obviously, they were not passed on to anyone following him. Elisha followed Elijah as a prophet in Israel. Elisha became the leader and prophet but did not have the keys of the Melchizedek Priesthood. Elijah did not confer the priesthood keys upon Elisha. When Elijah was taken up by a chariot of fire, his protégé, Elisha, saw him go and by a previous promise, Elisha received a double portion of the spirit of Elijah[389] and he did many miracles. However, that double portion did not include the priesthood sealing keys which Elijah took with him.

It appears from this discussion that Israel was not righteous enough to be worthy of the special temple sealing ordinances that are provided by the keys held by Elijah. All of Israel following Elijah including the prophets did not have the opportunity to have a temple marriage performed while in mortality because the sealing keys were taken by Elijah.

We should not be confused with Elijah's taking the sealing keys from the earth, with the special powers given to the prophet Nephi by the Lord[390] just prior to the birth of the Savior.

Nephi was extremely dedicated and righteous and was given a special power to call the people to repentance. This power was not the keys

---

[387] 1 Kings 19:14
[388] 1 Kings 19:16
[389] 2 Kings 1-14
[390] Helaman 10:4-11

that Elijah held. The keys Elijah held are only conferred by the laying on of hands. Nephi's power was not given by the laying on of hands as did Elijah to Joseph Smith and Oliver Cowdery. It was declared by the Lord to expand Nephi's existing priesthood powers. The following is the declaration of the Lord to Nephi, who was the leader of the Nephite people prior to the Savior's coming to them.

> *Behold, thou art Nephi, and I am God. Behold,* **I declare it unto thee** *in the presence of mine angels,* **that ye shall have power over this people, and shall smite the earth with famine, and with pestilence, and destruction, according to the wickedness of this people.**
>
> <u>Behold, I give unto you power, that whatsoever ye shall seal on earth shall be sealed in heaven; and whatsoever ye shall loose on earth shall be loosed in heaven; and thus shall ye have</u> **power among this people.**
>
> *And thus, if ye shall say unto this temple it shall be rent in twain, it shall be done.*
>
> *And if ye shall say unto this mountain, Be thou cast down and become smooth, it shall be done.*
>
> *And behold, if ye shall say that God shall smite this people, it shall come to pass.*
>
> *And now behold, I command you, that ye shall go and declare unto this people, that thus saith the Lord God, who is the Almighty: Except ye repent ye shall be smitten, even unto destruction.* [391]

Some read the underlined portion of this quote without understanding the bolded portion of this quote. The power that he was given was to bring destructive events on the Nephites. This destructive power was given to Nephi because he would use it to give judgments to the wicked that they might repent. He was a high priest using his Melchizedek priesthood to perform these miracles. He did not have or need the sealing keys for temple ordinances to perform these miracles.

---

[391] Helaman 10:6-12

Joseph Smith clearly stated that Elijah took these sealing keys with him into heaven. Elisha did not have the sealing power because there was no laying on of hands to give that power to him, yet he performed many miracles by his Melchizedek Priesthood.

What Priesthood Authority Remained?

After Elijah, what priesthood would have remained? We have to go to modern revelation to get the answer to this question. The Lord had this to say about the office of high priest,

> *High priests after the order of the Melchizedek Priesthood* **have a right to officiate in their own standing, <u>under the direction of the presidency</u>**, *in administering spiritual things, and also in the office of an elder, priest (of the Levitical order), teacher, deacon, and member.* [392]

High priests can "*officiate in their own standing*" but under the "direction of the presidency." When Elijah was in mortality, he had the priesthood keys which made him the "president" of those who held the Melchizedek Priesthood. Having left mortality with those keys, there was no president. You have to have the keys of the priesthood to be President. Those holding the Melchizedek Priesthood after he left would be high priests because they are the only ones who could "*officiate in their own standing*."

It should be noted that a stake president functioning as a high priest in his own ministry can ordain others as high priests, elders, priests, teachers and deacons. However, he cannot ordain bishops in the same manner. The President of the Church has to approve someone to be ordained a bishop[393]. Note that the office of bishop is not listed in the offices that a Stake President can ordain on his own. With no "President" no bishops would be ordained.

Elisha held the office of high priest. After Elijah, all the prophets would have been ordained high priests. Lehi being a prophet was a high priest. Lehi was not a Levite but held the Melchizedek Priesthood. He did not hold the temple sealing keys because those temple keys were not had in Israel at that time. Consequently, since Elijah was taken up to heaven none of the prophets in Israel held

---

[392] D&C 107:10.

[393] D&C 68:18-19 (14-20).

these keys. If Elijah had performed the marriage covenant for others during his mortality that ordinance would be effective for the participants. However, following his departure there was no one who could perform that ordinance with proper authority.

The Dilemma – No Sealing Keys

Since the temple sealing keys were taken away by Elijah all the prophets following Elijah were not married by the marriage covenant. This means that Isaiah, Daniel, Jeremiah, Ezekiel, Lehi, Nephi, Jacob, Alma, King Benjamin and many other prophets of the Old Testament and of the Book of Mormon were not married in the new and everlasting covenant or marriage covenant during their mortality. They held the office of high priest in the Melchizedek Priesthood and could qualify for the new and everlasting covenant (marriage covenant) but no one on the earth had the priesthood keys to perform the ordinance.

At first reaction one might say this could never be! These prophets exercised great leadership and received many visions and made prophecies some of which apply to our day. They did marvelous things in the name of God. We revere these prophets greatly and admire their deeds and faithfulness. How could they be deprived of the marriage covenant?

The purpose for taking the keys from Israel appears to relate to the general wickedness of the Israelites. It would appear that the prophets and what few other righteous people would be denied this most holy ordinance but that is not the case. They just did not receive it in their mortality. Regardless of the reason that the Lord took the sealing keys from the earth that is what the Lord did. Joseph Smith confirmed that he took those keys with him. They did not remain on earth following Elijah.

These faithful Israelites will not be denied the marriage covenant blessing. These prophets and others like them lived faithfully to the full extent of the gospel law that was available to them and have fulfilled all that they were able to do. They have earned the right to the marriage covenant. However, that ordinance must be performed on their behalf. As we know in our dispensation that we research our ancestors and perform these ordinances on their behalf. The Lord will see that these ordinances will be completed for these dedicated and righteous prophets and their spouses.

As one thinks on these things, they need to answer this question: "Does it really matter in eternity whether they receive the priesthood and temple ordinances including the marriage covenant in mortality or by proxy?"

The Solution

We should not be disturbed that these righteous prophets were not married by the sealing keys of the Melchizedek Priesthood during their mortality. Other good and holy men have lived on this earth to fulfill righteous and holy missions. Not all of them were members of the Savior's church during their mortality. One group of such men and women were born to make the United States free and independent with a constitution of guaranteed freedoms.

Wilford Woodruff had this to say about these men and women shortly after experiencing a visit from them while he was the President of the St. George Temple. He described that visit at a conference shortly following their visit to him,

> *I will here say, before closing, that two weeks before I left St. George, the spirits of the dead gathered around me, wanting to know why we did not redeem them. Said they, '**You have had the use of the Endowment House for a number of years, and yet nothing has ever been done for us. We laid the foundation of the government you now enjoy, and we never apostatized from it, but we remained true to it and were faithful to God.**' These were the signers of the Declaration of Independence, and they waited on me for two days and two nights. I thought it very singular, that notwithstanding so much work had been done, and yet nothing had been done for them. The thought never entered my heart, from the fact, I suppose, that heretofore our minds were reaching after our more immediate friends and relatives. I straightway went into the baptismal font and called upon brother McCallister to baptize me for the signers of the Declaration of Independence, and fifty other eminent men, making one hundred in all, including John Wesley, Columbus, and others; I then baptized him for every President of the United States, except*

three; and when their cause is just, somebody will do the work for them. [394]

Brian H. Stuy compiled additional information from the journal of Wilford Woodruff and the St. George temple records relating to this event which was published in the Collected Discourses, volume 3 in the appendix of that book. At the beginning paragraph in the appendix, he wrote,

No vision received by Wilford Woodruff is more well known than the appearance of the Signers of the Declaration of Independence. This vision, received "two weeks before leaving St. George," prompted Wilford Woodruff to compile a list of prominent men and women of the seventeenth and eighteenth centuries. On 21 August 1877, Wilford Woodruff, assisted by John Daniel Thompson McAllister (St. George Stake President), David H. Cannon (son of President George Q. Cannon) and **Lucy Bigelow Young (plural wife of President Brigham Young), performed the baptismal work for the one hundred seventy-one names on his list.** *He* <u>then called on the Saints of St. George</u> **<u>to perform the endowment and sealing work, which was accomplished by February 1878</u>**<u>.</u>

He continued quoting Wilford Woodruff as writing the following,

When Br. McAllister had Baptized me for the 100 Names I baptized him for 21, including Gen. Washington & his forefathers and all the [Preside[n]ts of the United States that were not in my list. Except [Buchannan [,] Van Buren & Grant.

Of the sisters, he wrote,

Sister Lucy Bigelow Young went forth into the font and was Baptized for Martha Washington and her family and seventy (70) of the Eminent women of the world [baptisms were performed by John Daniel Thompson McAllister, with confirmations by William Fawcett] [395]

---

[394] Young, Journal of Discourses Vol 19, P 223
[395] Stuy, Collected Discourses 3: Appendix

President Wilford Woodruff again talked of this event in the fourth day of the April 1898 Church Conference in the second afternoon session during which he said,

> Brother Cannon has been laying before you something with regard to the nation in which we live and what has been said concerning it. I am going to bear my testimony to this assembly, if I never do it again in my life, that **those men who laid the foundation of this American government and signed the Declaration of Independence were the best spirits the God of heaven could find on the face of the earth. They were choice spirits, not wicked men. General Washington and all the men that labored for the purpose were inspired of the Lord.**
>
> Another thing <u>I am going to say here, because I have a right to say it. Every one of those men that signed the Declaration of Independence, with General Washington, called upon me, as an Apostle of the Lord Jesus Christ, in the Temple at St. George, two consecutive nights, and demanded at my hands that I should go forth and attend to the ordinances of the House of God for them.</u> Men are here, I believe, that know of this, Brothers J. D. T. McAllister, David H. Cannon and James G. Bleak. Brother McAllister baptized me for all those men, and then I told these brethren that it was their duty to go into the Temple and labor until they had got endowments for all of them. They did it. Would those spirits have called upon me, as an Elder in Israel, to perform that work if they had not been noble spirits before God? They would not.

Several general authorities have quoted and emphasized this bolded quote of President Woodruff showing how noble and great these people were. Ezra Taft Benson talked of this work in the November 1987 Church Conference in his talk entitled "Our Divine Constitution." He emphasized that these people were great men and women, some of the best that God could find.

He further explained that,

> **President George Washington was ordained a high priest at that time. You will also be interested to know that, according to Wilford Woodruff's journal, John Wesley, Benjamin Franklin,**

and Christopher Columbus were also ordained high priests at that time. [396]

These above quotes were cited to show great men, the signers of the constitution and the other men and women fulfilled the charge that God gave to them even though they were not members of his Church. Yet these people had earned the right to have their temple work and sealings completed. They demanded it of Wilford Woodruff because they had served God in what they did.

There is another group of such holy men, not specifically identified, whom the Lord is reserving to himself. The Lord said,

Wherefore, I will that all men shall repent, for all are under sin, ***except those which I have reserved unto myself, holy men that ye know not of.*** [397]

Who these holy men are and what they have accomplished or will accomplish is not known. We can be assured that they will have served God in their accomplishments and will be rewarded accordingly with all the eternal blessings that we have.

PETER DENYING CHRIST

Why Peter denied the Savior during the night of the Savior's condemnation and maltreatment has been baffling to many people. Peter knew that the Savior was the Messiah and yet he denied knowing the Messiah three times. The Savior had this exchange with his Apostles and Peter

He saith unto them, But whom say ye that I am?

And Simon Peter answered and said, Thou art the Christ, the Son of the living God.

And Jesus answered and said unto him, Blessed art thou, Simon Bar-jona: for flesh and blood hath not revealed it unto thee, but my Father which is in heaven. [398]

The Savior clearly confirmed to Peter that the Father had revealed this truth to him. A little later as the Savior, Peter, James and John

---

[396] Benson, Teachings of Ezra Taft Benson P 604
[397] D&C 49:8
[398] Matthew 16:15-17

were returning from the Mount of Transfiguration, where they had seen Moses and Elias, a special witness was given to them.

> *While he yet spake, behold, a bright cloud overshadowed them: and behold a voice out of the cloud, which said, This is my beloved Son, in whom I am well pleased; hear ye him.*
>
> *And when the disciples heard it, they fell on their face, and were sore afraid.* [399]

A careful review of the scriptures reveals that even though Peter and the other apostles had witnessed his divinity they did not know what the mission of the Messiah really was and therefore their witness and understanding was incomplete.

In order to understand Peter's denial, we need to go to the Scriptures and show what his real understanding was about Jesus Christ being the Messiah.

Messiah Understanding

It is common knowledge that the nation of Israel wanted to shed the Roman rule. The best scriptural example showing the common attitude is when the Savior appeared to Cleopas and a companion as they traveled from Jerusalem to the village of Emmaus. The Savior was unknown to them. A conversation followed and Cleopas talked of,

> *...Jesus of Nazareth, which was a prophet mighty in deed and word before God and all the people:*
>
> *And how the chief priests and our rulers delivered him to be condemned to death, and have crucified him.*
>
> **But we trusted that it had been he which should have redeemed Israel"**[400]

What Cleopas was saying was that since Jesus of Nazareth was crucified and died, he couldn't redeem Israel from the Romans! The expression "we trusted" was speaking of the followers of Jesus of Nazareth who believed he was the Messiah. But he had died and now

---

[399] Matthew 17:5-6, Mark 9:5-7, Luke 9:33-35
[400] Luke 24:19-21

he couldn't redeem Israel from the Romans. They were still under Roman rule.

The experience of Peter, James and John accompanying the Savior to the Mount of Transfiguration gives further clues as to the mindset of the apostles. When all was done and on their way down the mount the Savior told Peter, James and John

> *he charged them that they should tell no man what things they had seen,* **till the Son of man were risen from the dead.**
>
> *And they kept that saying with themselves,* **questioning one with another what the rising from the dead should mean.**[401]

They did not know anything about a resurrection. Understanding the resurrection was not a part of the Jewish culture at that time. Although we understand it, his apostles did not understand it prior to the Savior's actual resurrection. The concept of the Savior dying and then being resurrected is fundamental to knowing the mission of the Messiah. There was no common knowledge of these concepts in Israel at the time.

Following Peter's first stated testimony that Jesus was the Son of God the scriptures record

> *From that time forth began Jesus to shew unto his disciples, how that he must go unto Jerusalem, and suffer many things of the elders and chief priests and scribes, and be killed, and be raised again the third day.*
>
> *Then* **Peter took him, and began to rebuke him, saying, Be it far from thee, Lord: this shall not be unto thee.**
>
> *But he turned, and said unto Peter,* **Get thee behind me, Satan: thou art an offence unto me: for thou savourest not the things that be of God, but those that be of men.**[402]

Here we have the Savior begin to teach his apostles and followers what would shortly come to pass and Peter rebuked the Savior. He clearly understood that the Savior was talking of his death. Peter said

---

[401] Mark 9:9-10
[402] Matthew 16:21–23

"this shall not be unto thee." He was the Messiah and he was going to deliver Israel from the Romans. He should not die.

The Savior rebuked Peter for his comment actually calling Peter "Satan"

> *Get thee behind me, Satan: thou art an offence unto me: for thou savourest not the things that be of God"*[403]

This rebuke did not change Peter's mind. At the Last Supper, the Savior said this to Peter

> *I have prayed for thee, that thy faith fail not: and* **when thou art converted, strengthen thy brethren.**
>
> *And he said unto him,* **Lord, I am ready to go with thee, both into prison, and to death.**
>
> *And he said,* **I tell thee, Peter, the cock shall not crow this day, before that thou shalt thrice deny that thou knowest me.** [404]

This exchange is very important to understand. The Savior was trying to teach Peter to be prepared to strengthen his brethren. This suggests that Peter needed to be ready to take the lead with his brethren. Peter's mindset was that he was going to follow the Savior. He was

> *ready to go with thee,* **both into prison, and to death.**"

This is a significant statement by Peter when in a matter of a very short time the Savior would be arrested. Peter was ready to defend the Savior and to die defending him if necessary. This shows that Peter would be quick to use his sword in the Savior's defense. His motivation was his belief that the Savior would redeem Israel from the Roman rule. The Savior could not do that if he was dead.

The Savior responded with his prophecy of Peter denying him three (3) times. When the Savior told Peter that he was not yet converted, the Savior knew that Peter did not understand that the Savior's mission was to die and provide the resurrection for all of humankind. The Savior had already told his disciples of his impending events that he must suffer and Peter did not understand. He did not understand but he was ready to fight.

---

[403] Matthew 16:23
[404] Luke 22:32-34

For that matter, none of the other apostles understood his resurrection. Peter was not alone in his lack of understanding. Mark records this about the apostles' reaction when they were told of his resurrection.

> *And they, when they had heard that he was alive, and had been seen of her, believed not.*
>
> *After that he appeared in another form unto two of them, as they walked, and went into the country.*
>
> *And they went and told it unto the residue: neither believed they them.*
>
> *Afterward* **he appeared unto the eleven as they sat at meat, and upbraided them with their unbelief and hardness of heart***, because they believed not them which had seen him after he was risen.* [405]

They had no concept of the resurrection. They could not understand that the Savior would be living following his death. When Peter and John ran to the sepulcher the Savior was not there,

> *Then went in also that other disciple (John), which came first to the sepulchre, and he saw, and believed.*
>
> *For as yet they knew not the scripture, that he must rise again from the dead.* [406]

Peter Defending the Savior

Following the Savior's Garden event, the group came to arrest the Savior. The following was recorded by Matthew,

> *And, behold, one of them which were with Jesus stretched out his hand, and drew his sword, and struck a servant of the high priest's, and smote off his ear.*
>
> *Then said Jesus unto him,* **Put up again thy sword into his place: for all they that take the sword shall perish with the sword.**
>
> *Thinkest thou that I cannot now pray to my Father, and he shall presently give me more than twelve legions of angels?*

---

[405] Mark 16:11-14
[406] John 20:8-9

> *But how then shall the scriptures be fulfilled, that thus it must be?* [407]

All four gospels give a similar story that one disciple took a sword and cut off the ear of the servant of the High Priest. John identifies that disciple as Peter.

At the beginning of the arrest Peter now executed his mindset and his personal commitment of protecting the Savior. He reacted immediately taking his sword and swung it at the head of the high priest's servant. Striking at the head is the kind of blow that would kill or do serious injury. But Peter only cut off the ear whereupon the Savior healed the servant's ear and chastised Peter for using his sword telling him that those who use the sword will die by the sword.

The Savior chose to tell Peter that he could have more than twelve (12) legions of angels because it described far more angels than the Romans had soldiers. He chose the term legions because it mentally links angels against the soldiers. Using the term "twelve legions of angels" emphasizes that the Savior did not need to rely upon Peter for his safety. The message was that he had the power to crush the Romans without Peter's help.

This was a severe chastisement to Peter. This was his Messiah whom he knew was the Messiah by revelation and by the voice of the Father. He had seen heavenly messengers with the Savior. He was helpless to protect the Savior. This exchange had to have caused Peter to be extremely unsettled concerning what to do. He had been so firm and hot in his commitment of defending the Savior and then chastised so strongly.

The Savior's mission had to be fulfilled. But Peter did not understand what that mission was. Following this exchange, the Savior willingly placed himself into the hands of this arresting group. The arresting group showed great fear of the Savior when they came to arrest him.

> *Jesus therefore, knowing all things that should come upon him, went forth, and said unto them, Whom seek ye?*
>
> *They answered him, Jesus of Nazareth. Jesus saith unto them, I am he. And Judas also, which betrayed him, stood with them.*

---

[407] Matthew 26:51-55

> *As soon then as he had said unto them, I am he,* **they went backward, and fell to the ground.**
>
> *Then asked he them again, Whom seek ye? And they said, Jesus of Nazareth.*
>
> *Jesus answered, I have told you that I am he: if therefore ye seek me,* **let these go their way:** [408]

Peter watched the arresting group react to their fear of the Savior. This group knew of his miracles and feared him because they did not know whether the Savior would use miracles to do harm to them. Peter witnessed this fear by the soldiers. He also understood the Savior's comment to "let these go their way." He was in this deep quandary but he got the message that he <u>must not be</u> with the Savior. The other disciples fled. Peter was still concerned about the Savior and followed at a distance trying to be discreet. By being discreet he felt he could remain unknown and avoid being associated with the Savior and yet observe what would happen.

It should be noted that the Savior was arrested after dinner and relatively early in the night. [Read the section DETERMINING PASSOVER EVENTS at Page 180 for the justification that it was fairly early in the evening].

We cannot place the time of the first two denials with exactness but they probably happened during the Savior's maltreatment. Matthew records Peter's first denial as follows,

> *Now Peter sat without in the palace: and a damsel came unto him, saying, Thou also wast with Jesus of Galilee.*
>
> *But he denied before them all, saying, I know not what thou sayest.*

The damsel challenged Peter directly. Here Peter did not exactly deny that he was with Jesus. His response was to plead ignorance by saying *"I know not."*

> *And when he was gone out onto the porch, another maid saw him, and said unto them that were there, This fellow was also with Jesus of Nazareth.*

---

[408] John 18: 4-8

> *And again he denied with an oath, I do not know the man.*

Here the maid accused Peter of being with Jesus to the others who were present. He had tried to minimize the first challenge but now the charge was stronger and made in his presence to the crowd around him. For fear of being punished as the Savior was being punished, his response was stronger by saying *"I do not know the man."*

> *And after a while came unto him they that stood by, and said to Peter, Surely thou also art one of them; for thy speech betrayeth thee.*
>
> *Then began he to curse and to swear, saying, I know not the man. And immediately the cock crew.* [409]

Now the crowd was accusing him of being a disciple. Peter responded more strongly by cursing and denying the charge.

Peter witnessed many events throughout the night beginning with the arrest in early evening. In addition, he milled among the other spectators hearing their verbal exchanges. The Savior was condemned to die. He witnessed or heard of the Savior being buffeted with fists, slapped with their open hands, spit upon, mocked and beard pulled out[410], This is not recorded in the New Testament but was prophesied in Isaiah. This act was done to shame the Savior. They mocked him by covering his head, striking him on the head and then telling him to prophesy who struck him. This continued for some time. Peter witnessed that the fear of the arresting group changed to vicious maltreatment. He knew he should not be caught up in this situation.

His faith was not fully developed at this time because he did not understand the true mission of the Savior. He previously showed that lack of faith when he feared while walking on the water.[411] As he began to sink into the water, the Savior took him by the hand and said *"O thou of little faith, wherefore didst thou doubt?"* He was severely chastised by the Savior and the events of the night caused him some fear. He witnessed the fear of the arresting party and the resulting

---

[409] Matthew 26:69-74

[410] Isaiah 50:6

[411] Matthew 14:28-31, JST Matthew 14:24-25

attitude of brazen and harsh maltreatments. Then the cock crowed and Jesus turned to look at Peter.[412]

His love for the Savior was very great. He had a revelation that Jesus was the Son of God and heard the Father's voice confirming that Jesus was the beloved Son of the Father. This was the man who would not let the Savior wash his feet because he thought the Savior should not humble himself to do this lowly activity. Upon learning that he without this could have no part of the Savior, he wanted hands and head washed.[413] His desire and love was strong, but he had let the Savior down. He had denied knowing the Savior three times. This was a devastating realization for Peter and he wept bitterly because he had failed the Savior. This reaction shows Peter's great and driving love for the Savior.

Being Converted

On the morning of the resurrection the women went to the tomb to complete the preparation of the body for final burial and were told by the angel that the Savior had risen. They reported this to the apostles who ran to the site. Luke records this

> *Then arose Peter, and ran unto the sepulchre; and stooping down, he beheld the linen clothes laid by themselves, and departed,* **wondering in himself at that which was come to pass.** [414]

Previously Peter did not understand about the resurrection and the need for the Savior to die. He was beginning to get the picture as he began his "wandering." When Mary Magdalene reported to the apostles that she had seen the Savior, they doubted her.[415] Their doubt was removed when Cleopas returned to Jerusalem to report to the apostles, they had seen the Savior and that he lived.

According to Luke the Savior then appeared to the apostles and Cleopas and his companion.[416] They were able to see and feel the scars from the nails. The risen Savior taught them and their

---

[412] Matthew 26:75, Luke 22:61-62
[413] John 13:4-14
[414] Luke 24:12
[415] Mark 16:9-10
[416] Luke 24:33-36

understanding developed. They walked together to Bethany and then the Savior left them. Peter was converted! He Knew! Peter and the others finally understood the resurrection and the message and they rejoiced in it. The Savior had been resurrected and had provided the atonement for humankind. Peter went forth with boldness, understanding and conviction to lead Christ's church because he finally understood the true mission of the Messiah.

When the Savior told Peter "when thou art converted, strengthen thy brethren"[417] He was really saying "When you understand my mission, strengthen thy brethren." The term "converted" as used by the Savior requires that one come to the correct knowledge and understanding of the Savior's mission. Peter knew Jesus was the Messiah by revelation and by the Father's words but had not understood what the mission of the Messiah really was.

DETERMINING PASSOVER EVENTS

The Savior ate the Passover dinner with his apostles and probably other disciples. We know the Passover day is observed in the spring time and begins in the early evening because the Jewish day starts at dusk and ends the following evening at dusk. The significance of the Passover celebration is in recognition of Jehovah cursing the Egyptians by taking the life of their firstborn children while he preserved the firstborn of the Israelites, as recorded by Moses. This was done to persuade the Pharaoh to release the Israelites from Egyptian bondage.

> *Then Moses called for all the elders of Israel, and said unto them, Draw out and take you a lamb according to your families, and kill the passover.*
>
> *And ye shall take a bunch of hyssop, and dip [it] in the blood that [is] in the bason, and strike the lintel and the two side posts with the blood that [is] in the bason; and none of you shall go out at the door of his house until the morning.*
>
> *For the LORD will pass through to smite the Egyptians; and when he seeth the blood upon the lintel, and on the two side posts,*

---

[417] Luke 22:32

> the LORD will pass over the door, and will not suffer the destroyer to come in unto your houses to smite [you].
>
> And ye shall observe this thing for an ordinance to thee and to thy sons for ever.
>
> And it shall come to pass, when ye be come to the land which the LORD will give you, according as he hath promised, that ye shall keep this service.
>
> And it shall come to pass, when your children shall say unto you, What mean ye by this service?
>
> That ye shall say, It [is] the sacrifice of the LORD'S passover, who passed over the houses of the children of Israel in Egypt, when he smote the Egyptians, and delivered our houses. And the people bowed the head and worshipped.[418]

The lamb's blood being spread upon the doorposts and crossbeam was the requirement that would preserve the firstborn of the Israelites. The significance of this celebration was to remember the preservation of the Israelites. Unbeknown to the Israelites, because of the things he would suffer, this Passover day would be the preservation of not only Israel but of the whole world. It had great significance to the Savior.

This section is to estimate the time of the sunset, dusk, dawn and sunrise of the Passover day at the end of the Savior's earthly ministry. Understanding these things will help us to understand more fully what and how long the Savior suffered through that night and the following day.

We assume because of the consistency of the planetary system that the sun will rise and set as times on the day of Christ's Passover are the same or within minutes for the same calendar day for 2016.

From the internet, the beginning dates for Passover for a number of past years was identified. They varied from late March to late April. The date of April 10 is chosen as that is the date that Passover will start in 2017 and seemed to be near the middle of the dates. Assuming this to be the equivalent date for the Savior's Passover we can now determine the time for dawn and dusk for that date.

---

[418] Exodus 12:21-27

Obviously, this is not the exact date, however, it is within minutes of the actual time for the Savior's Passover.

A table at "timeanddate.com" shows Jerusalem's times for April 2016[419]. The times in this table are daylight savings times. Since there was no such thing at the time of the Savior the times are adjusted to reflect the actual time. That table contains the following information:

DATE	TIME	EVENT/COMMENT
April 9	6 pm	Party arrival
April 9	Dusk 6:29 pm	Passover start - Candles lit
April 9	6:40 pm	Dinner started
April 9	7:20 pm	Judas leaves – Conversation, Peter prophecy, Intercessory Prayer
April 9	8:30 pm	Gethsemane - Garden suffering
April 9	9:30 pm	Judas arrives – Savior arrested
April 9	10:15 pm	Trial - Maltreatment Events
April 10	Dawn 5 am	Cock Crowed, Peter's response

These estimates are offered because the author believes the Savior suffered the maltreatments for a considerable time through the night which added to his fatigue and eventual suffering from the entire affair.

The three gospels although using slightly different language state that when it was time they sat down to eat. It is likely that they arrived prior to the lighting of the candles. A likely time for the starting of the meal would be very soon following dusk. The meal would have lasted perhaps two (2) hours. The actual eating perhaps forty-five (45) minutes to an hour with some conversation following. It could have been shorter.

---

[419] http://www.timeanddate.com/sun/israel/jerusalem?month=4&year=2016 Last visited July, 2020

The Savior identified Judas Iscariot as his betrayer early during the meal. Matthew records the Savior as verbally identifying Judas following the dipping.

> *Then Judas, which betrayed him, answered and said, Master, is it I? He said unto him, Thou hast said.*[420]

The latest that Judas left was probably before the end of the meal. He left to initiate the arrest of the Savior.

The chief priests, scribes and elders met with Caiaphas to consult how they could arrest Jesus in secret. They feared the reaction of the people if they saw the arrest.[421] Judas had met earlier with this group with an offer to deliver the Savior for arrest out of the public view. They agreed on 30 pieces of silver.[422] Judas knew the place where the Savior and apostles often went after their meals which was a Garden across "the brook Cedron"[423].

This arrest being preplanned would not take a large amount of time to implement. It took perhaps an hour and a half or probably a little less from the time that Judas Iscariot left the meal to gather the arresting party and return to the Garden. So somewhere about 2 hours from the start of the meal Judas would be at the Garden.

The next crucial question is "How long did the Savior suffer in the Garden? His suffering would last as long as it took to eliminate all of the blood from his body.

He shed from every pore large drops of blood that lasted perhaps thirty (30) minutes or a little shorter. As soon as all of his blood was eliminated, he would be released from Satan's torment relieving his pain. There would be no purpose to suffer longer.

The arresting party came soon after the Savior had completed his Garden ordeal. The arrest probably took place about 9:30 pm. This would allow two hours for Judas to gather the arresting group and go to Gethsemane. The trial before Caiaphas probably started about 10:30 pm. The point of this discussion is to show that before the cock crowed Peter would have witnessed the trial, death sentence and

---

[420] Matthew 26:25
[421] Matthew 26:3-5
[422] Matthew 26:14-16
[423] John 18:1-2

maltreatment that the Savior suffered. The maltreatments excluding the scourging would have concluded about the time that the cock crowed.

John records

> Peter then denied again: and immediately the cock crew.
>
> Then led they Jesus from Caiaphas unto the hall of judgment: and **it was early**;[424]

The meeting with Pilate probably started about 6:00 am. It was a short time following the cock crowing that they left to travel to the hall of judgment.

The point of this discussion is that the maltreatments by the soldiers lasted some 6 – 8 hours. The Savior endured this ordeal keeping his promise to the Father. He was perfect in his commitment.

■ ATONEMENT PERSPECTIVES ■

This book was developed to explain some of the thoughts about the Savior's atonement and related scriptural events and issues. It is not a complete book covering every question or issue. It is hoped that it will give the reader a better understanding of what and how our Savior accomplished his mission. In accomplishing his mission, he always followed and accepted the will of the Father.

However, to qualify for eternal life one does not have to understand everything about the atonement of the Savior and every subject discussed in this book. It requires simple faith in him and his teachings and commandments and living a life like the Savior and enduring to the end of their life.

But we must consider what Joseph Smith said

> And if a person gains more knowledge and intelligence in this life through his diligence and obedience than another, he will have so much the advantage in the world to come.[425]

---

[424] John 18:27–28
[425] D&C 130:19

Best Wishes to you in this endeavor to gain more knowledge and intelligence.

■ BIBLIOGRAPHY ■

Backman, Milton V., Jr., Ed, *Regional Studies in Latter-day Saint church history: Ohio*; [Provo, Utah], Dept. of Church History and Doctrine, Brigham Young University; 1990.

Benson, Ezra Taft. *The Teachings of Ezra Taft Benson.* Salt Lake City, UT: Bookcraft, Inc., 1988.

Bible History Online. *Bible History Online.* http://www.bible-history.com.

Church of Jesus Christ of Latter-Day Saints. "*The Family: A Proclamation to the World.*" http://www.lds.org/topics/family-proclamation?lang=eng.

Church of Jesus Christ of Latter-day Saints, Seventy-Eighth Semi-Annual Conference Report, Salt Lake City, Utah, Oct 1907; http://www.scriptures.byu.edu/gc-historical/1907-O.pdf.

Church of Jesus Christ of Latter-day Saints, Ninety Ninth Annual Conference Report, Salt Lake City, Utah, April 1929; http://www.scriptures.byu.edu/gc-historical/1929-A.pdf.

Dictionary.com, LLC. *Dictionary.com.* http://www.dictionary.com.

Gospel Doctrine, Sermons and Writings of Joseph F. Smith, Salt Lake City, Utah, Deseret Book Company Inc., 1939

History of the Church, 6 Vols, can be viewed at

https://byustudies.byu.edu/history-of-the-church

What, Andrew F., and Lyndon W. Cook, comps. *The Words of Joseph Smith: The Contemporary Accounts of the Nauvoo Discourses of the Prophet Joseph Smith.* Provo, Utah: Religious Studies Center, Brigham Young University, 1980.

The Free Dictionary, http://www.newworldencyclopedia.org/entry/Info:Main_Page

Journal of Discourses. 26 vols. Liverpool: F.D. Richards, 1855-86. [Brigham Young verbally authorized George D. Watt, who was skilled in stenography, to take his notes to England and publish them. Both felt that these publications could not be published in the United States because of the anti-Mormon sentiment. Each volume was entitled "Journal of Discourses" with the year of publication which contained the previous year's records. The first nineteen volumes were listed, "by President Brigham Young," signifying his verbal authorization for publication. The last seven volumes were listed, "by President John Taylor." David W. Evans and George W. Gibbs later assisted and continued in this work of publishing]

McConkie, Bruce R. *The Mortal Messiah*. 4 vols. Salt Lake City, UT: Deseret Book Co., 1979.

Merriam-Webster, Inc – An online dictionary: http://www.merriam-webster.com

New World Encyclopedia, A Free Online Encyclopedia, http://www.newworldencyclopedia.org/entry/New_World_Encyclopedia:About

Smith, Joseph. *History of the Church of Jesus Christ of Latter-Day Saints*. Intro and notes by B. H. Roberts. 7 vols. Salt Lake City, UT: Deseret Book Co., 1948.

Smith, Joseph Fielding. *Church History and Modern Revelation*. 4 vols. Salt Lake City, UT, Deseret Book Co., 1946. [These books were authorized as the Melchizedek Priesthood course of study for the years 1947-1950, and were approved by the Quorum of the Twelve Apostles.]

Stuy, Brian H., ed., *Collected Discourses*, 5 Vol., Woodland Hills, B. H. S. Publishing, 1987.

Talmage, James E. *Jesus the Christ*. Salt Lake City, UT: Deseret Book Co., 1983.

Whiston, William, A.M., Trans. *Complete Works of Flavius Josephus*, Grand Rapids, Michigan, Kregel Publications. Josephus Writings are also available online at http://www.sacred-texts.com/jud/josephus/index.htm.

Wikimedia Foundation, Inc. *Wikipedia: The Free Encyclopedia*. http://www.wikipedia.org.

Zias, Joe "Crucifixion in Antiquity", Century One Foundation. http://www.centuryone.org/crucifixion2.html. Article no longer available at this site, but is archived by Internet Archive Wayback Machine at http://web.archive.org/web/20110615201341/http://wwwcenturyone.org/crucifixion2.html.

www.ingramcontent.com/pod-product-compliance
Lightning Source LLC
Chambersburg PA
CBHW060826050426
42453CB00008B/599